W9-AMB-124

THE ART OF
INTIMACY
THE PLEASURE OF
PASSION

A Journey into Soulful Relationship

by

MEL SCHWARTZ

QUANTUMPRESS

Quantum Press 1999

Copyright ©1999 Mel Schwartz. All rights reserved.

Printed and bound in the United States of America.

Book design by Windy Waite.

No part of this book may be reproduced or transmitted in any form
or by any means, electronic or mechanical, including photocopying,
recording, or by an information storage and retrieval system—except by
a reviewer who may quote brief passages in a review to be printed in a
magazine or newspaper—without permission in writing from the
publisher. For information, please contact Quantum Press, P.O. Box 490,
Chappaqua, N.Y. 10514.

Although the author and the publisher have made every effort to ensure
the accuracy and completeness of information contained in this book,
we assume no responsibility for errors, inaccuracies, omissions, or any
inconsistency herein. Any slights of people, places or organizations are
unintentional.

Library of Congress Cataloging-In-Publication Data

      Schwartz, Mel

The Art of Intimacy, The Pleasure of Passion/Mel Schwartz

      p. cm.

      ISBN 0-9670110-0-1

           99-093064 CIP

DEDICATION

I dedicate this book to my parents, Ruth and Sid. Their marriage of fifty-five years has been a celebration of loving intimacy and passion. They have been the inspiration for my vision, and their encouragement to be who I am, gave me the courage to live my truth.

I also thank my children Alex and Jesse, whose love encouraged me during this writing.

And I offer my deepest gratitude to all those souls whom I have met and loved along the way.

PREFACE

As a psychotherapist and in my personal life, I am often confronted with a very disheartening picture: Many relationships that begin with the greatest of hopes fade into mediocrity. The loftiness of love withers; it becomes ordinary. Too often the wonderful visions of an intimate life become clouded by the inevitable resignation to joyless relationships.

I have encountered much heartbreak and too many unrealized dreams. I've been witness to the dulled conversations and the acceptance of love-less and passion-less lives. And I am saddened by what I see, for I know there is a loving potential in our soul that remains hidden just beneath the surface. The solutions await us, if we only know where to look for them.

My quest has been to create a new way of relating that enables people to nourish and successfully love one another. I believe that the answer to our longing for a more complete happiness lies in our ability to awaken our consciousness, permitting us to rewrite the script of our lives.

I am inspired by those who have transformed their lives in this manner, as they have embarked upon the path of insight, opening to the unfolding of joy. When we devote ourselves to intimacy and passion, our lives thrive. The ability to move beyond our fears and obstacles frees us to enjoy the riches of intimate relationships. We all deserve the treasure of loving intimacy. This book is devoted to that purpose.

CONTENTS

Information About the Author

To inquire about other books, audio or video products, or to learn about speaking and seminar appearances by Mel Schwartz, you may either call 914 238-6835 or visit our website at THEARTOFINTIMACY.com. We welcome your comments, which may be mailed to:

Quantum Press
P.O. Box 490
Chappaqua, N.Y. 10514

Quantity discounts are available on bulk purchases of this book for educational or fundraising purposes.

The Art of Intimacy, The Pleasure of Passion is also available as an audiobook.

INTRODUCTION

The voice of our soul informs us that we should be bathed in the splendor and warmth of loving arms and gentle caresses. We long for the bliss of unconditional love and we fantasize about the ecstasy of profound intimacy and exquisite passion. We want to share our lives with another soul who understands us and loves us beyond limits. This was how life was supposed to be.

Yet, too often our relentless quest for such fulfillment is met with disappointment. We may have become frustrated and disillusioned. In fact, we may have given up on our earlier dreams of wonderful and joyous relationships.

As young adults we likely had hopes of great love and intimacy. We dreamed of the fullness a rich love life might provide; however, as life went on we may have come to resign ourselves to less. The earlier vision of a wondrous life remained beyond our grasp.

Most of us long for more intimacy and passion in our lives. These are essential requirements for a happy life. Still, we struggle in that pursuit. The problem may lie in the fact that we were never trained in the Art of Intimacy. Enlightenment about our personal relationships is the pathway to happiness. Enjoying sustained intimacy and passion require insight and a new way of being in a relationship.

When we were children we studied English, history and math. We were educated and trained for the purpose of becoming responsible, mature people, capable of productive lives and successful careers. Our childhood was a preparation for what we thought was to be a happy life.

However, one very important subject omitted from our curriculum was the Art of Intimacy.

We were never schooled in the subject of relationship. There weren't any lessons on the subject of intimacy, or how to have and sustain a fulfilling relationship. The very cornerstone of a happy life was glaringly missing from our education. Why weren't we taught how to fulfill our dreams, choose appropriate partners or deal honestly with our feelings? Wouldn't it have been helpful to understand techniques that foster intimacy and keep passion alive?

This journey remains uncharted because no one taught us. The dominant model for relationship was our parents. They may have said that they wanted us to be happy, but they never taught us how. No one ever taught them, and so the cycle continued.

With this lack of training we focused outward. We thought that happiness would just happen. But joyous relationships don't just happen. No matter how successful or accomplished we may be, achievements in other areas cannot compensate for the pain caused by conflicted or failed relationships. The foundation for happiness lies in our relationships. Success and achievements are simply adornments that may very well enhance our lives, but cannot substitute for the absence of a healthy base.

Yet, we remain illiterate in the field of relationship. This is the one essential thing that we all need, but,...no training. It seems absurd, doesn't it?

As Erich Fromm said in his acclaimed book *The Art of Loving*, "In spite of the deep seated craving for love, almost everything else is considered to be more important than love: success, prestige, money, power, almost all our energy is used for the learning of how to achieve these aims, and almost none to learn the art of loving."

This deficit haunts our lives, contributes to the divorce rate, and is a fundamental cause of depression, anxiety and addiction. The absence of nurturing relationships leaves most of us emotionally famished. Our hunger for meaningful fulfillment leaves us wanting for more. And so we often turn to addictive behavior to quiet the pain.

The plague of our times is called depression. This malady of our culture is more the norm than the exception. People in depression feel isolated, removed from others. The isolation stems from a lack of harmony and fulfillment. Intimacy with oneself and others is missing.

There is often a misconception that true intimacy is unattainable. Physicians monitor our serotonin levels as though that is the cause of our depression. It might be wise to consider that our serotonin levels are affected by our state of relationship. What we feel is manifested in our blood chemistry, not caused by it.

People in intimate and passionate relationships don't feel depressed or become addicts. That is where people turn in their pain. We resort to the drug to dull our aching hearts and quiet our souls, which yearn for so much more. Medication, overwork, overeating or addiction cannot compensate for our lack of loving intimacy. We are indoctrinated to think that happiness will come with our next foray into consumerism and material acquisition. The solution lies elsewhere. We must return to the source and lovingly provide each other the nourishment that we long for.

THE MYTH

We study throughout our schooling to achieve better grades so that we might have good jobs and successful careers. We are ready to learn all that is required to succeed in life. Our preparation is never ending. Twenty years of academic education is quite ordinary. And yet not a single moment is spent enlightening us about happiness and intimacy. We honor intellect and material success, but we suffer in our relationships because no one ever taught us. And most of us go through life depressed by our disappointments, feeling that it's our fault. We believe that others are happier in their relationships. The tendency is to mask our shame or humiliation, feeling that we are somehow less worthy than others. The fault lies not with us, but with a social system that has subverted our priorities.

This feeling of inadequacy is an intrinsic piece of a pernicious myth. This myth tells us that others are happier, that our incompleteness is unique to us. The belief is that we don't quite measure up. We feel flawed. Internalizing this myth is terribly destructive to our self-esteem. The myth becomes a self-fulfilling prophecy.

If we could unburden and share our insecurities with one another, then we wouldn't have to bury our anxieties behind the facade of pretending that we're okay. With the possible exception of an enlightened guru, no one is quite there. Doubt and imperfection are simply part of being human.

The myth, however, tells us that we are damaged. We are, almost without exception, all suffering, all wanting something better. We are simply in various stages of the journey. The quest for happiness and fulfillment has typically left us short of the goal.

Another facet of the myth is that being in a relationship, in and of itself, will provide joy. This myth takes on enormous proportions when we consider the institution of marriage. As young adults we are led to believe that our lives will be wonderful simply by being in a relationship, and even more so, in marriage. Regrettably, most marriages are unhappy. At least half end in divorce and it would be naive to assume that the majority of intact marriages are necessarily joyous. Only a small percentage of relationships actually thrive. This represents a staggering rate of failure. Why do we permit this? We would never tolerate this failure in our businesses. *Indeed, if marriage were a corporation it would be bankrupt.*

It is the very system of relationship that produces these devastating results. We can no longer seek excellence in our careers and permit such mediocrity in our personal lives. Marriage, and its myth of happiness, is for the most part masked in illusion.

The facade of defensive posturing must be penetrated if we are to transform our lives. We must eliminate the cultural myth that others are happier. It is liberating to realize that it is not our own personal failure but that we are part of a system of relationship that isn't succeeding. To enter into relationships and play by the same rules that produce this failure rate is simply unconscious. It is akin to sleepwalking. If we are to make intimacy and passion a priority in our lives we need to awaken and shift how we see relationships.

To achieve this, we must open to one another in all our truth and vulnerability. Whenever I share this belief with others I perceive an immediate unburdening. People are immensely relieved when they realize that they are not alone. It is human to have doubts and insecurities and it is our humanness that must serve as our ally into joy and love.

PARADIGM SHIFTING

In order to transform our relationships we need a new paradigm. A paradigm is a dominant belief system. It is comprised of assumptions and beliefs about the truth of what is. It structures the way that we see things and ourselves. The dominant paradigm influences not only what we think, but also how we think.

Moreover, our personal beliefs are ordinarily a mirror of the existing paradigm. The tendency is to accept such a belief system unquestioningly. We equate them with being the truth. Yet, once we begin to consider what we had previously left unexamined, our reality alters. Truths and myths shift as old ground breaks into new.

The old paradigm of relationship was that happiness would simply happen. No insight or training was necessary. Intimacy and passion would simply flow from the partnership and we would be happy ever after. If you didn't succeed in your relationship the message was that there was something wrong with you, or your partner.

Much energy was devoted to maintaining this belief. If you

didn't feel such happiness, it was your fault. This paradigm was well illustrated by the 1950s television show, *Father Knows Best*. That popular TV series made it clear that all we have to do is get married, have kids and buy a house to enjoy a wonderful life. This mental model had an unstated principle. You didn't need any training or devotion to relationship; it would just take care of itself.

The old paradigm of relationship honors the form of relationship, but ignores the content. It dishonors the deeper needs of our soul—love, nourishment, intimacy and passion. The message was that anyone who was not happy needed to be fixed.

Labels, such as dysfunctional, were attached to people and families. People are not dysfunctional; social systems are. People suffer and experience pain. We are human beings, not machines that dysfunction. Such terminology expresses utter contempt for the human spirit. A social system that inculcates conformity and utilizes fear as a socializing tool is dysfunctional.

We are corralled into a consensus of belief that does not serve our higher purpose. Still, most would rather fit into the molded expectations of proper lives than strike out on our individual journey into life's pleasures. Why is this? It's because we are afraid. We are more afraid of making a mistake than we are of living purposeless lives. We are the products of a culture that ignores and devalues matters of the heart, creates malaise and then turns and points its accusatory finger at those who suffer. This is madness.

These rules of relationship cause us to lose our inner voice so that we hear only the beliefs of the system at large. The old paradigm suppresses the cries of our souls. You should be happy it instructs, and if you're not, there's something wrong with you. It is a system devoid of soul that envelopes itself in the hypocrisy that it calls family values. Family values ought to be love, intimacy, wonder, spirituality and joy—not greed, conformity, duty and fear.

The old paradigm dishonors truth. We instruct our children to tell the truth and then we proceed to model truth-less lives. We receive the message that it is unwise or inexpedient to be truthful with others. Living one's truth is subordinated to the greater goals of accomplishment. Expressing our truth becomes conditional to the circumstances at hand. Sharing honestly might upset the relationship or jeopardize our career or simply subject us to the judgments of others. The fear of not fitting in compels us to forsake our truth. When we dishonor our truth, we lose our souls. We detach from our purpose and go through life more asleep than awake. Our lives become depressed and without higher purpose. Intimacy and love cannot prevail in the absence of truth.

I recently watched a television interview with the baseball superstar Mark McGwire as he approached Roger Maris' home run record. He said that breaking the record didn't matter to him, helping his team win was what counted. Who could possibly believe this statement? His team was playing abysmally and had no chance of making the playoffs. Most of the nation was thrilled by his astonishing performance. In this circumstance, McGwire was fashioning a selfless team player personality for himself. But he wasn't sharing the truth. And in his case the truth was absolutely blameless. Just consider how we behave when we think others will fault us.

Genuine truthful exchange of authentic meaning becomes the exception. We become so inured to the deadness of our words that we turn off. We talk at one another but we don't exchange our hearts or our being. This process induces us to lose our inner voice, our inner truth. And it anesthetizes our relationships.

The new paradigm places relationship first. It is one that honors love, intimacy and joy, above all else. These blessings will not flower into our lives without an unburdening and a commitment to sharing our truths. Authentic, joyful relationship must be the foundation for a happy life, not a coincidental by product. It is mindless to place all of our energies on education, knowledge, and successful careers, and ignore the very foundation of happiness.

A major shift in priority must be the essential ingredient in recreating our relationships. *The Paradigm Conspiracy* proposes a threefold process for shifting paradigms: 1) confronting pain 2) waking up our souls 3) reclaiming our innate creative powers. All of these elements are intrinsic to finding genuine intimacy in our lives.

The new rules of relationship acknowledge, without judgment, that disappointment and pain have been the norm, not the exception. It elucidates with kindness that the child is ever present in the adult and that fear and doubt are often constant companions.

Happiness and fulfillment are part of a commitment to a continual process devoted to intimacy and truth, love and passion. This emerging paradigm calls on us to discover a new path, illuminated by an awakening consciousness. Once we have freed ourselves from our illusions we can emerge from the darkness and take responsibility for who we are and consciously create joyful lives.

The Art of Intimacy, The Pleasure of Passion is a guide into joyous relationship. We will uncover the obstacles to intimacy and move beyond the fears that restrict us. We'll practice new techniques for relationship that will awaken our hearts and open us to soulful relationship. The flow from intimacy into passion is inexorable. They are parts of the same current. Passion does not have to die. The belief that it will is a self-fulfilling prophecy. If you believe it... it will happen. We'll discover a new way of seeing, as we rewrite the rules of relationship. We can create partnerships that flourish, in which intimacy is the ingredient and passion is the pleasure that follows. Loving intimacy and passion are our birthright.

Chapter 1

HAPPINESS

THE FROG

The parable of the frog is particularly helpful in illuminating the nature of relationships. If you place a frog in a pot of boiling water, the frog will immediately recoil from the heat and jump out of the water. It instinctively feels the danger and chooses to survive. It's a very different story if you place the frog in a pot of lukewarm water and slowly start to heat the water. It adapts to the rising temperature and the frog endures the increased heat and becomes lethargic. Eventually the frog loses the will to leave the boiling water and is scalded to death.

This is often where we find ourselves in our relationships. We become acclimated to the toxic environment and mediocrity. We grow accustomed to the absence of joy and pleasure. Much like the frog, we may lose the initiative to leap out of the scalding water and thrive. If we knew at the start of the relationship that it would evolve in this manner we would likely not have begun. This parable also applies to our own inner relationship. As with the outer relations, we become all too familiar with mediocrity and we may lose our vision.

Endurance and obligation are not the fruits of relationship. They are the instruments of guilt and fear. A relationship must serve our highest purpose if we are to thrive. The length of union that has turned mediocre, or worse, is not a justifiable reason for the continuance of that drudgery. Happiness is the product of intimacy, not duty. Joyful relationship, replete with intimacy and passion, can emerge with an awakening of consciousness. The process starts with a clearer understanding of the nature of happiness.

I'LL BE HAPPY WHEN...

Intimacy is described as characterizing our deepest nature, reflecting our true essence. It is a sharing of our most authentic nature. In order to have an intimate relationship with another, we must first know deeply of ourselves and then share in that profound knowing with our partners. It is in this knowledge that happiness will be found. This is a happiness that is not fleeting or contingent upon external events or factors. The foundation for intimate relations with others is a profound, non-judgmental knowledge of oneself. For we certainly can't be intimate with another if we aren't intimate with ourselves. With this self-intimacy we are prepared to enter into intimate relations with others. So it would seem only natural that the first steps toward happiness would begin with the path toward developing intimacy, first with ourselves, and then with our partners. But we get side tracked right from the start. To better understand what happens, let's explore our understanding of happiness.

In our culture happiness is generally seen as a future event. It usually depends on something else happening. I'll be happy when... The script goes something like this:

I'll be happy when... I get married.

I'll be happy when... I get my promotion.

I'll be happy when... we buy our dream house.

I'll be happy when... we furnish the house.

Still, we find happiness is elusive, so we put it off in anticipation of the next milestone.

I'll be happy when... we have children.

I'll be happy when... the children are grown.

I'll be happy when... we retire.

What has happened here? An entire lifetime has passed. Were the visions of happiness just a fantasy, an unattainable illusion?

> *Life is what's happening while you're busy making other plans.*
> —John Lennon

The problem is twofold. First, happiness is being based on a future event, and second, our expectations are that we will derive our inner joy from an external happening. Both perceptions are founded in a mythic illusion.

The future is a present that we have not yet lived. Reality exists only in the instant of this particular moment. The question we must ask ourselves is, what must I change this instant to achieve my bliss? Since this moment is about to pass into the next, the formula for happiness must be found within oneself in the present moment or it will be forever lost in the fantasy of the future. If we reflect upon our past expectations of happiness, we will see that once our desires were filled, we simply substituted new ones. Happiness will only be realized by achieving a loving intimacy in the present.

A particularly articulate young woman who recently attended one of my workshops told the following story. She described her marriage as simply being alright. She referred to it as a safe and comfortable environment, but she and her husband lacked a deep connection. She admitted that there was an absence of intimacy and a lackluster sex life. It was not the marriage that she had really hoped for, but it was good enough, she said, to get by. She convinced herself that it was unrealistic to expect better.

After ten years of marriage she had begun to acclimate to the absence of love and nourishment and had become somewhat groggy, like our friend the frog. She compensated for her emotional deficits by looking outwards. Since her husband was on a financial fast track, she assumed that the dream house they were to buy would bring her the fulfillment she needed. She poured her attentions in that direction. Shortly after they had purchased the house she put her promise of happiness into the decorating of the home. This too served as a temporary fix, only to be replaced by other goals that would produce the elusive happiness. She was spending her life chasing after the illusion of happiness. Her relational disquiet was being suppressed in a vain attempt to seek external comfort. Eventually she turned to alcohol to quiet her turmoil.

We can see that she was looking outside of herself and her relationship for happiness. It won't be found there. The tendency is to focus on the events and plans in our lives and to put our energy there, rather than focus on our internal joy. When we do so we are guaranteeing an exercise in futility.

EXTERNALIZING

Very often, romantic relationships culminate in the ritual of marriage. For young people the institution of marriage promises to be a safe haven. Two young people, who likely have not examined their own lives too deeply, join in the promise of a happy life. Any self-exploration or deeper considerations of the relationship are ordinarily turned outward.

No sooner does the couple decide to become engaged then they place their energy on the plans and goals of the wedding. They may barely know one another on a deeply intimate level, yet they already begin to turn away from each other. The dance of intimacy has already begun.

Their thoughts are directed toward the honeymoon, the bridal and bachelor parties and of course, the wedding plans. I would conjecture that much more time is spent on these details than on the state of their relationship. They likely busy themselves with thoughts about who is on the guest list and what are the seating arrangements. The more important concerns are neglected. What are our visions for a life together? What are our fears and concerns? What issues do we need to work through? Questions such as these are typically avoided for fear of upsetting the apple cart.

When I counsel people considering divorce, I often ask them why they decided to marry their spouse in the first place. Their responses are, at times, oddly quizzical: "Well, I knew there was a problem from the start but the invitations were already in the mail," or "I didn't want to disappoint my family." As incredible as it may seem, the plans have taken precedence over the relationship itself.

The sanctity of the marriage is already being dishonored. The commitment is to the form of the relationship, not the content. This turning outward is what I refer to as externalizing. And it continues.

The focus on the events and goals becomes a panacea for the fact that there isn't genuine happiness in the moment. This is because happiness is being sought in the wrong place. I have often heard people refer to their homes with the expression, "the house needs work." How much better might it have served them to say, "our relationship needs work"? They may refer to the life they have built together. What have they actually been building: friends, vacations, possessions? Have they been committed to a life of intimacy and passion? Have they been sharing their dreams and their fears? Do they go to sleep at night with thoughts inside their heads that they don't share with their partner?

The fact is that they have not been building a life together. By the time they come to realize this they have accumulated many years of frustration and resentment. At this point they may resemble our frog in the boiling water, wondering how they ever got to this point.

Chapter 2

THE SHADOW

---

*Your relationship with another is always a
mirror of your relationship with yourself.*

WHY OPPOSITES ATTRACT

Although most of us enter into romantic relationship out of a desire
for love, there is an underlying and compelling need to join with
another. In all likelihood, we haven't ventured deeply into our journey of self-exploration. Moreover, as young adults we are faced with
the daunting task of replacing our family of origin. The tacit message in our culture is that it's not okay to be alone. We're led to
believe that a relationship, or better still, marriage, will provide the
security and comfort that we're searching for. So we begin our quest
for fulfillment in our search for a mate. But too often we marry for
the wrong reasons. Marriage becomes the rite of passage. We feel
more adult-like because we have a partner in betrothal and we can
now present ourselves as complete.

To illustrate this point in our development, it might be helpful to
think of yourself as a half moon. As a half moon there is a sense of
oneself, yet there is a fundamental lack of completeness. We feel as
though there is an essential piece missing and we therefore seek out

another half moon in an attempt to become whole. This is a quick fix, of course. The alternative is to remain unattached and go through the travails of our own inner exploration in the hope of reaching a deeper, more profound sense of our own self-intimacy. A few choose this course. But more often we take the easier route of merging with another. The latter choice provides an instant sense of relief and so we usually choose this option.

So why do our relationships suffer and fail as often as they do? Primarily because joining with another out of neediness is a prescription for failure. Any relationship that is built upon compensating for your needs by attaching to another will not work. This is not to suggest that you must spend your life alone. Far from it. Relationship provides the opportunity for incredible pleasure and comfort. But we must know ourselves more deeply if our relations with others are to be less reactive and more fulfilling. Typically the union of two people who have not come to know deeply of themselves will serve only as a temporary resting place for their individual turmoil. Eventually the tempest will spill over onto the relationship.

MY OTHER HALF

Let's take a deeper look at this phenomenon so we can understand the process. We're familiar with the expression opposites attract. To understand why opposites attract let's go back to the consideration of the half moon. The moon is of course always full; it's just that light illuminates only half of it. For now, let's call the dark side "the shadow."

The shadow represents that part of your identity that is hidden from sight. The shadow contains the traits that are opposite of your visible personality. For example, if you pride yourself on being a generous person, the shadow contains the propensity for being stingy. If you are passive, your dark side is domineering and assertive. So, to carry this analogy a bit further, a half moon has a tendency to join with another half moon who reflects their opposite traits. In this manner the moon completes itself, becoming whole.

Typically, the other person's personality characteristics will be similar to those contained in your shadow. That is why opposites attract. The expression "my other half" can be taken quite literally. It is for this reason that we find givers coupling with takers, aggressive people matched with passive partners and insensitive individuals pairing with highly sensitive counter parts.

The story of Judy will help this theory come to life. Judy, a woman in her early thirties, had always had an issue with her shyness. She was a particularly intelligent woman who was nonetheless frustrated by her inability to overcome her diffidence and interact with others in a confident manner. She married in her mid-twenties and, not surprisingly, Judy married a man who was exceptionally outgoing. She was unconsciously attracted to a man who possessed a persona opposite of her own, or similar to her shadow. She was literally completing a part of herself by merging with her opposite. Judy dealt with her deficit, by joining with a gregarious man. She had chosen the simple path. She was compensating for her deficiency by acquiring that characteristic from her partner.

In therapy, Judy began to explore her shadow, including her problem with shyness. She began to assert herself more appropriately and eventually overcame her difficulties in this area. Judy began to deal with others in an effective and forthright manner. As she did so her relationship with her husband began to shift. The very thing that initially attracted Judy to him now began to repel her. She came to view her husband as lacking in discretion and being somewhat inappropriate. He was, of course, the same man that she was originally attracted to. It's just that she no longer needed him to fill her void, so she began to see him quite differently. Judy eventually decided to dissolve her marriage and rewrite the script of her life. If she continued to move toward her own wholeness, she would improve the likelihood of finding fulfillment.

From this example we can see why joining with another to complete a deficit of our own is likely to fail. As soon as one person grows in some manner, their needs shift and the relationship becomes unbalanced. We begin to see our partner in a different light and they may no longer suit us. When our needs change, our expectations shift and the love energy of our relationship is affected. We may come to see that love, when based upon satisfying our needs, rests on very shaky ground.

Until we examine our shadow, we are unaware of its existence. Yet, the majority of our behavior emanates from this unconscious area. In other words, we aren't even conscious of why we are attracted to whom we are. That's a startling piece of information. We are not making conscious and considered choices about whom we choose as a partner. It's small wonder that our relationships suffer as a result. We are being unconsciously drawn to the other in an attempt to complete ourselves.

The solution is to come to know more deeply of ourselves. The union of two people who have not looked sufficiently into themselves will likely be just a temporary resting place from their individual unrest. Our relationships with others always mirror our relationship with ourselves. If we have not explored our shadow, it will cast its image onto our partners. We literally project the highly reactive shadow component onto our partner in an attempt to displace our own disquiet. As long as we see them as the source of the problem, we cannot evolve toward our own wholeness or enjoy the pleasure of intimate relationship.

BRINGING THE SHADOW INTO THE LIGHT

Two people in a relationship, who are unconscious of their shadows and have not begun the process of self-examination, are likely to blame the other for what might be their own issues. The very things that they find themselves reactive to are really their own problems. Yet, they fault their partner. This creates a relationship rife with conflict.

The way through this dilemma is to bring the shadow into the light. When you feel your button being pushed by your lover, realize that it is your button. Ask yourself, Why am I feeling what I am? When you feel yourself reacting negatively to another, shift your focus away from them and ask yourself, "What is triggering this response in me?" The source of your reaction to another will be found within your own shadow. We must look inside of ourselves and stop blaming others for our unhappiness. If they don't suit us we must come to examine why we selected to be with them from the outset. The answer will reveal fully what is likely buried in our shadow.

Barbara and Bill's struggle clearly demonstrates the powerful influence of the shadow on our relationships. During their marriage of fifteen years, Barbara had exhibited a strong tendency to be self-interested and had difficulty nurturing others. Barbara had a difficult time seeing beyond her own needs. Bill's personality was, not surprisingly, rather different. He was very self-sacrificing and giving. When he came home from work he would prepare dinner for the children and get them off to sleep. Barbara had full-time, live-in help and didn't work. Yet, she assumed little responsibility in caring for the children.

For many years Bill looked the other way. He claimed that Barbara's traits didn't really bother him. She was free to enjoy herself he suggested, however, as time went by Bill started to become reactive and resentful. A struggle ensued in which Barbara and Bill began faulting one another. Bill began to criticize Barbara for her selfishness and Barbara, being rather narcissistic and not open to self-reflection, lashed out at her husband in return.

I helped Bill look inside of himself rather than project his anger outward toward Barbara. After all, Barbara was essentially the same person that Bill had fallen in love with and had chosen to marry. So I asked Bill, "Why did you choose this woman to marry?" Bill was nonplussed as he struggled to answer the question. As we began to explore his shadow, Bill searched within to find that part of him that needed to take care of himself before anyone else. This was not a part of Bill that he was comfortable with, and it remained buried in the darkness. Our trigger point with another reflects what is locked away in our own shadow. Therefore, he had become very reactive to that proclivity in his wife. Barbara's inclination to immerse herself in her own neediness infuriated Bill precisely because he didn't permit himself any part of that characteristic.

Ironically, it was likely that this very trait in his wife had accounted for much of his original attraction to her, albeit unconsciously. Something was shifting in Bill. He was losing his capacity to respect his wife. Since Bill's inclination to care for himself remained in his shadow, it was highly charged. As he uncovered this shadow component, Bill was able to take a look at his own needs for self-gratification and modify his behavior accordingly. As he did, he found that he was less reactive to Barbara's behaviors. Bill's shadow had greatly impacted on his behavior. He had unconsciously been attracted to a woman who exhibited traits that were buried within his shadow.

Once Bill learned to take responsibility for his feelings and make considered and conscious choices about his relationship, he no longer permitted his buttons to be pushed by his wife's behavior. Bill might eventually decide that his relationship with Barbara isn't in his best interests, but this conclusion would now come from an enlightened choice, rather than an unconscious reflex of blame. It is likely that if he had done some shadow exploration before his marriage, he might never have married Barbara.

At times people wonder what to do with shadow components that don't suit them. For example, a person who is generous might protest that they have no desire to become stingy. That is completely understandable. The exercise of shadow integration calls for the nonjudgmental acknowledgement that the characteristic exists. In other words, there lies beneath the surface a propensity toward that trait. But we don't need to reflect that trait in our personality. Simply bringing it into the light serves to make us more conscious and less reactive.

THE TRIGGER POINT

Taking responsibility for oneself is fundamental for developing intimacy. When another person triggers us we must ask ourselves, "What part of me is being reactive?" Let your partner serve as a mirror into yourself. This is one way in which our relationship facilitates greater self-awareness.

In fact, when things get heated, try this technique: In the midst of an argument, imagine a mirror between your partner and yourself.

Whatever you are saying to your partner say to yourself. The words must be addressed to your own shadow. If you find yourself saying to them, "I hate you, you're so selfish," consider your own feelings about selfishness. What is it in the other person's behavior that you could not tolerate in yourself? Look into your shadow and see if you can find that trait hidden in the darkness.

There is a wonderfully simple exercise that can help you come to know your shadow. Make a list of all of your known personality traits. This list should include features of your personality you recognize in yourself and that others see in you. Enumerate these features in a vertical column. Across from every trait list your concept of the opposite characteristic.

The list of opposites you have identified represents your shadow. It is here that you are triggered by others and act unconsciously. The more highly reactive you are to particular features of your partner, the deeper that characteristic is buried in your shadow. Bring these features into the light and you are on the road to awakening and intimacy.

When you feel your button being pushed you must take a very deliberate and conscious time-out. Your trigger is in reflex mode and if you pull it, you cannot maintain the detachment necessary for witnessing your thoughts and actions. And you cannot possibly feel love. You'll be lost in the argument, reducing your capacity for self-reflection. When we use the expression *my button* the emphasis must be on the word *my*. Your partner has catalyzed a reaction in you that requires that you look into your own self and ask, What is it that

I see in them that I could never tolerate about myself?

By taking this bold step forward to embrace your own individual responsibility, you are opening the door to intimacy. By developing authentic intimacy with ourselves we may then do the same with our partners. If we continue to see the problem as being the other's, the enemy being out there, nothing will change. By venturing down the path of self-exploration, we can enter into conscious choices about our partners and ourselves.

ONE SOUL, TWO GENDERS

Understanding the impact of the shadow is fundamental to developing healthy relationships. In particular, gender differences are exacerbated by a lack of integration of shadow self. The Mars-and-Venus view, which highlights the differences between the sexes, is somewhat simplistic.

A more spiritual approach to personality development embraces the idea that as humans we are all, most essentially, souls. As souls, we know no gender. We are both feminine and masculine, having experienced all possible forms. We have lived many lives in the sexuality of both genders.

Typically, our personality is identified with our gender. Therefore, the stereotypical man has his feminine side buried in his shadow. He typically needs to attach to a woman to compensate for his lack of femininity, which is hidden in his shadow. Paradoxically, he is also triggered by her womanhood, for he is usually uncomfortable with this aspect of himself. So the male in our culture tends to resist the openness and heart center of the woman. The female may present emotional and intuitive aspects of herself that provoke reactive responses from her logic-oriented male partner.

Conversely, the female may be dependent upon her masculine mate for his appearance of strength and rationality. Yet, this perspective leaves both in a very needy place. Each may resent the other for having what they need within themselves. This is a primary cause of the manipulative power struggles between men and women. This neediness contributes weightily to conflict and unhappiness in relationship.

Identifying and attaching to the label of one's gender is self-limiting and soul defeating. Focusing on the immutable differences between the sexes and commercializing on the conflict is opportunistic. An intrinsic law of the universe is that balance is to be found within all systems by the harmony reached between integrating opposites. The Oriental terminology for this phenomenon is yin and yang. Yin represents feminine energy, soft, yielding and nurturing. The masculine yang is assertive and domineering. A healthier balance can be reached within one's self by acknowledging their opposite gender found in their shadow.

Men and women attempt to complete themselves by pairing with their opposite gender, but as we have seen, friction often arises. The evolution of our souls requires that we identify and integrate our shadow, which includes our other sexuality. When man no longer needs woman to nurture him, but can do so for himself, and when woman no longer needs man to protect and support her, but can do so for herself, we have a relationship that is open to prosper and flourish. For it is the absence of neediness that permits unconditional love to emanate. A man who has evolved toward his wholeness by accepting his feminine shadow, and a woman who has actualized by developing her masculine side, are much more likely to enter into a mature and intimate relationship.

What we refer to as love is really often need. If you have gone without food for a long time and are overcome by hunger, it is likely that you will eat whatever is available. It won't matter much if it suits you or is good for you. You will fill yourself with whatever is available. But, if your meal is on time and you aren't overwhelmed by hunger, you might consciously select from the menu and choose more reasonably. And so it is with relationship. When the energy of a relationship is based upon conscious attraction and mutual enhancement, rather than filling a void, joy and fulfillment may arise.

THE PARADOX

Surprisingly, what at first glance would appear to be logical contradictions, can be a powerful tool for creating healthy relationships. Whatever it is that you desire to change about your partner, exemplify in yourself. If you want him to be more supportive, the best way to accomplish that is to be more supportive yourself. If you want her to be less critical, be less critical yourself. Nobody wants to be told to change their behavior. Indeed, most people actively resist any such suggestion. Yet, we typically continue to tell our partner what he or she needs to change. The more that we do so, the less likely it will occur. As soon as they perceive a criticism, the more defensive they become. The wall goes up and the argument begins. All opportunity for meaningful exchange is lost, and the desired change becomes but a wishful thought.

By employing the paradox, or the opposite interaction, we free the other from the defensive resistance we created. The expression, "If you do what you've always done, you'll get what you've always gotten," typifies the futility of demanding change from another. It never works. The paradox is, therefore, to do the opposite of what we have typically done. As we proceed on the journey into intimacy, we will come to see that paradoxical behavior often produces the result that we're in search of.

Randy and Linda came to see me on the verge of ending their seven-year marriage. Linda complained that Randy didn't act as a partner in their marriage, he was too concerned with his own needs. She felt ignored and unappreciated. Randy protested that Linda was overly critical and was always telling him what to do. He felt as if he needed her permission all the time. He said his independence and self-esteem were called into question. Randy wanted Linda to be less critical and wished for more of a supportive relationship. Linda wanted her husband to be more involved with her life. The reality was that their demands were driving them away from one another.

Linda's need for Randy's attention inclined her to be critical of his behavior. The more hostile she became, the more judged Randy felt, and the more he moved away from Linda, exacerbating the situation.

Their needs were serving to repel them from each other. In fact, the paradox is that the only way they may get what they want is to do the opposite of what they've been doing. If Linda released Randy from her expectations he might feel less criticized. If that happened, he'd be much more likely to want to be with her and provide her with the partner that she desired. So if Linda, in fact, became the partner that she wanted Randy to be, he would feel less attacked and more open to providing her with what she was looking for.

The more they insisted upon change from their partner, the more defensive each became. Their behaviors locked them into positions that affected the opposite of what they claimed they wanted. The paradox is for them to behave in the manner that they want from their partner. If you desire a particular change from your partner, demonstrate what you want from them in your own behavior, rather than insisting that they change. Most people resist others attempts to change them. Changing another by making demands or offering threats is short-lived, at best. Change must be motivated from within. However, the irony is that by exhibiting the very quality that you are seeking from your partner, he or she is much more likely to shift.

Jeff came into counseling complaining of his frustrations with his eight-year-old daughter Chloe. Jeff had recently remarried and his extended family now included his children, his wife's children and the influence of two ex-spouses. They were all experiencing increased stress around adjustments to their new family system. In particular, Chloe was resisting all attempts to accommodate a new family structure. She identified strongly with her mother and saw her stepmother in an adversarial light. Chloe frequently acted in a disruptive manner and objected to all plans that included her new family members.

Jeff and his wife had planned an outing to a local amusement park and Jeff began to anticipate Chloe's refusal to join them. He was concerned that a major fight would erupt and that the trip would be ruined. As Jeff recounted how he had handled similar episodes in the past with his daughter, it became clear that the more he tried to induce reasonable behavior from her, the more she acted out.

I urged Jeff to try the paradox. I explained to him that the best thing to do was to explain to Chloe that he really wanted her to join the others at the amusement park and have a wonderful day, but if she didn't want to she was free to stay home. In other words, he could change his behavior. In doing so, Chloe would lose the opportunity to engage in hostile activity with him. There would be nothing for her to resist. Once Jeff removed himself from the conflict, Chloe's behavior would likely change.

Jeff did as I suggested and Chloe chose to stay home with a babysitter. Jeff reported that the following day, as he and his wife and the other children were making plans for another day of fun, Chloe actually asked if she could join them. He told me that this had never occurred in the past. It had always been a battle. By employing the paradox, Jeff created the results he desired.

In order to affect change in another we have to look to ourselves. By removing the limitations of controlling behavior, we allow our partners to disengage from the habitual patterns of resistance to change. The paradox is a very powerful tool in disengaging old patterns of behavior.

Chapter 3

Masks and Intimacy

You can't get from another what you don't give to yourself.

The word intimacy evokes different images for all of us; however, it seems that we'd all likely agree that whatever intimacy is, we'd all be better off with more of it. As I use the word, intimacy in a relationship refers to a very deep and profound honesty between two people. It is of the most genuine and authentic nature. To be intimate means that there are no disguises, that we aren't altering or modifying anything about ourselves. An intimate relationship requires that two people share their innermost being. The good and the bad. Anything short of that deprives the relationship of the intimacy needed for nourishment. If there is a part of yourself that you keep off-limits to your partner, you are dishonoring that person and the relationship.

Our relationships suffer and fail because of a lack of intimacy. One of the reasons we don't enjoy intimate relations with others is that we haven't yet discovered our own self-intimacy. You can't get from another what you don't give to yourself. To have intimacy with another requires that you first have an intimate relationship with yourself.

MASKS

As children we actually create our personalities. Although we may think of our personality as innate, much of it is manufactured. Major parts of our persona are creations born of our own neediness. The process of altering or modifying our true nature is very insidious. We are actually unaware that we are creating this personality. We usually fashion this false self in the hope that we will be more loved, more popular, smarter, prettier, and so on. In childhood we receive messages, overt or indirect, that we're not quite good enough. The news of our inadequacy typically comes from our parents, friends or relatives. The result is a place within us that is lacking, a void, an unhealed area. We think that if we could just change this or that, be different in some way, everything would be better. So we add additional layers to our original personality in an attempt to accomplish this goal.

I refer to these layers as masks. They cover and disguise our true being. Masks distance us from our soul, our true being. We create them out of a lack of self-love and self-esteem. The masks are projections from our own internal belief system. They come from the thought that we are not good enough just as we are. The mask separates us from our true nature. Therefore, the masks block us from intimacy with ourselves. Our egos, which identify with our personality, defend the masks, keeping them on, afraid of revealing our deeper nature, and so we find ourselves in a battle.

We can keep the masks with which we identify, or move more deeply into our true nature. This state of conflict creates a dissonance, which results in much upheaval. The struggle ensues as we feel these different components of ourselves vie for dominance. The personality, often rooted in fear, resists change and urges us to stop looking inside. The soul, ever expansive and in pursuit of our truth, propels us toward our true being. It might be helpful to think of this self-examination as a sort of growing pain. Others might refer to it as mid-life crisis. No matter what term we apply, it is growth.

Masks remove us from our partners and ourselves. They become the artificially created personality. Let's consider babies. Of course, babies don't wear masks. They have not yet learned to feign behavior or shift their personalities to get better results. When a baby is afraid, she cries. When adults are afraid they are likely to suppress the fear. They are apt to substitute anger rather than expressing their true feelings. Anger is a mask for fear. We are taught, and this is particularly true for men, that it is not acceptable to be afraid. Yet the emotion needs to surface. So we revert to the mask that we learned to substitute, anger. As long as someone wears the mask of anger, the fear will not surface. And the real issues cannot be addressed.

I was recently working with a couple in post-divorce treatment. They came to me to help them alleviate conflicts around their children. Susan's real concern was that the children preferred their father and were moving away from her. They balked at spending any time with their mother, and Susan blamed Tom for being the instigator of their behavior. She was terrified of losing her children, with all of the incumbent emotions around her sense of failure and abandonment. Yet, she clung to her anger. It was all her ex-husband's fault, she claimed. He poisoned the children against her, she protested. As long as she held tenaciously to her anger, it would mask her core emotion, fear. The angrier she became the more her children avoided her. But if she permitted the fear to surface she might be able to work through her real problem, her feelings of inadequacy as a mother.

Masks are always a product of fear. The mask creates a filter so dense that we lose sight of who we truly are. If we can't know deeply of ourselves, how can we have an intimate relationship with another? What is it that we'd be sharing, our false self? Masks are an obstacle to intimacy. They must be removed for intimacy to thrive. Self-love is the absence of masks, resulting in the unconditional acceptance of your true self.

VULNERABILITY OR STRENGTH?

Authentic strength flows from vulnerability. The conditioned personality assumes the aura of strength, all the while hiding from its fear. Again a paradox is revealed. Vulnerability, a condition many people regard as weakness, is in fact, strength. For the mask of strength covers the fear of self-disclosure. Those whom we refer to as having "big egos" are, in fact, highly defended and fearful. Wars are made by fearful men with big egos. The greater the mask, the greater the fear. We may have come to conclude that the appearance of strength is indeed desirable. Yet that mask requires much energy to defend it.

Ordinarily we define vulnerability as feeling exposed or open to hurt. It evokes a sense of weakness and fragility; however, once we have come to terms with our true self there is nothing left to defend. We no longer require approval from others and will not permit others to judge us. In this circumstance, vulnerability becomes a powerful ally. Once we are unmasked in our truth and vulnerability, there is no longer anything to fear. We have nothing left to hide. Love flourishes in our vulnerability.

The absence of the mask permits the true self to emerge. In order to be intimate with yourself, you must begin to unmask as you peel away the layers that you have accumulated in your false personality and go deep within yourself. You must be prepared to be kind and nonjudgmental, and accept whatever you find. If you're not, then you will continue to hide from yourself.

Unmasking is a very significant undertaking. Most of an unexamined life is spent avoiding such an exploration. However, greater self-knowledge is our inevitable destiny. So, as you start down this path congratulate yourself for having the courage to begin this journey. Unmasking places responsibility for the relationship squarely where it belongs, on your inner relationship. The outer relationship is always a mirror of your own inner relationship.

THE ROLES WE PLAY

The many different roles that we play later in life add even more layers of masks. Just consider the array: father, mother, child, employer, friend, sibling, homemaker. The list goes on and on. So complex becomes the maze of roles and masks.

First we have the childhood masks. Then come all of the roles that we play in order to function in the adult world. Often, we become so enmeshed in the role that we forget that it's simply a part that we play. We confuse the role with who we truly are. The actor, at the end of his performance, returns to his true identity. When the play is over he sheds the character.

For most of us, however, without an awakening of consciousness, we become our role. For example, the person who assumes the role of provider becomes so immersed in making money that he or she may forget that this is simply one of life's functions. Similarly, the caretaker may become so obsessed with nurturing others that the larger sense of self vanishes. In such circumstances our self-identity becomes aligned with the role that we play and our esteem is sought through this identification. There are numerous roles that we assume as we transition through different stages of life.

These roles create labels and identifications about who we are. They define our being, which is useful to an extent. The problem, however, is that they limit us as well. The roles imprison us within the limited constraints of prescribed behaviors. The provider who is so serious about his earnest responsibilities may lose his capacity for playfulness and innocence. The caretaker may overlook her own need to be nurtured. We become limited by the function we're performing and the joyfulness of our souls is forgotten. We are much more than the duties that we perform.

Very often the roles we assume become our justification for a lack of intimacy in our lives. We make excuses for not being present or available. In such cases our roles protect the masks that we wear. During a workshop I was conducting, Holly, a woman in her mid-forties, defended herself against her husband Ralph's complaints that their sex life was virtually non-existent. She rationalized that she was so weary from her duties as a mother and homemaker that she simply didn't have the energy for romantic and sexual relations with her husband.

I delved into this role with her, but she protested that she was, after all, a mother. That came first, and what could she do? I asked her about her parents and their relationship and we learned that her mother had disdained sex all together.

There was an underlying message that had been conveyed from mother to daughter. The message was that sex was to be shunned. A wanting sex life with her husband was being camouflaged by her responsibilities as a mother. Holly had retreated into her obligations as a mother to avoid dealing with a major issue in her life.

She was rather defensive about my attempts to open her to this perspective, so I tried a different approach. I told Holly to be the best mother she could be, she would have to be the best woman she could possibly be. Otherwise what would she be demonstrating to her children, a life devoid of passion and romance? They would likely inherit that legacy. Would she want her daughters to continue this cycle? Fortunately, Holly immediately responded to this insight. This approach motivated her to see that the mask she had adorned would impact heavily upon her children. Holly moved beyond the boundaries of her self-imposed role and opened to healing a fundamental wound.

UNMASKING

To achieve intimacy with your inner self, you must be prepared to accept and love the frightened child you're likely to find within. It is that child that created the masks to begin with. Your inner child must be brought into the light. To attain authentic adulthood, we must first grow back into our childhood. The adult must revisit the incomplete child and enter into a dialogue with it. The adult can now parent that child in a very supportive and nurturing manner.

The conversation that might ensue would have the adult acknowledge the child's pain and fears, and offer to join the child in a healing union. Through this dialogue the adult can now parent the child in a manner that might have been lacking originally. I suggest talking to your frightened child. Visualize your inner child and determine what age they are. Feel the fear and you'll know at once the age that you're stuck at. In your imagination join hands with the child and say that you're going to make it all right. You are there for them and the two of you can join in a loving way.

The acceptance of that vulnerable, frightened child is the first step in the unmasking process and the journey toward the emergence of your truc self. Those who do not take this path are likely to spend their lives looking for love and acceptance from others when, of course, it must first come from you. Someone else cannot truly love you if you don't love yourself. So the road toward fulfillment requires you to do the inner work. There is no shortcut.

Initially, we may not acknowledge that we wear any masks at all. However, if we search inward we are likely to find areas of falsehood that we try very hard to cover. Energy directed at covering this fiction results in the formation of a mask. And this produces relationships that fail or disappoint. The masks must come off.

If we choose to continue holding our partner at a distance, we are saying, "stay away, you can't come in here." We have two people in non-intimate relation with each other's masks. We dishonor them and they do the same to us. With that kind of equation, can there be genuine intimacy? And the years go by, and the water boils, and we wonder what happened to those great and optimistic beginnings that we shared.

Remember that intimacy requires the ability to look inside without any preconceptions about what we will find. The fear is that we may encounter a true identity altogether different from the personality that we've created. We are apprehensive that the person we'll find is different from the portrait we've painted. Most of us have unconsciously written the script of our lives very intricately and have worked hard to fashion the image that we call ourselves. Buried beneath that image, however, lies the true self. And it longs to be heard.

At times its cries may surface as anger, sadness or depression. It may manifest in bouts of irritability, anxiety or sleeplessness. Other times it's simply a subtle feeling that we are not being honest with our loved ones and ourselves. That cry is your soul pleading to be heard.

The measure of our discontent is the distance
between our personality and our soul.

The greater that distance, the less intimacy is available. The mask distances us from our inner being. It repudiates our soul. And it lives in fear. An unmasked personality permits the soul to shine through and radiate. In this way the personality is simply a reflection of the soul. In this manner we are in total harmony with our inner being. Only with this awakening can we become more conscious and enter into intimate relationships. Two people, committed to intimacy can co-create a wonderful life together. And one of the results of that experience is abundant passion. When you no longer expend all that energy defending your masks a new space opens for a loving, soulful expression of one's innermost being. That is the joy of relationship.

The first step toward unmasking begins with telling ourselves the truth. We must take an honest look at those little secrets that we've kept locked away. The secret is usually about a part of ourselves that we feel ashamed of, or a piece of us that feels inferior. We know the place; it's not quite authentic. So admit the secret to yourself. It needn't be a big one. You can start with small stuff; however what will unfold may be very large indeed.

JAKE

Jake was a man in his early forties who prided himself on his appearance. He looked much younger than his years and dressed to accentuate this fact. He usually wore Levi's, a tee shirt and a blazer. His hair was cut in a very contemporary fashion and he affected a somewhat rebellious look. During a therapy session he told me the following story.

Jake needed a new pair of shoes and so he went to the local mall to do some shopping. In the shoe store he found himself drawn to a pair of designer shoes, but he hesitated when he noticed that the shoes had a buckle. He felt that the shoes were not his look. He said that he had never worn a pair of shoes with a buckle; buckles were much too conservative, too mainstream he contended.

Curiously, he found himself unable to walk away from these shoes. He would look at them for a while, think about them, hesitate, walk away and then return. Jake said the entire experience felt bizarre. After a while he decided to try on the shoes. He walked around for a while, looked at them in the mirror and reported that this entire process bewildered him. Jake had always been a very spontaneous person. He made his decisions quickly. Surely something as simple as buying a pair of shoes didn't warrant such indecisiveness. Finally, he bought the shoes, though he still wasn't sure if he would wear them.

The dilemma of these shoes gave Jake an opportunity to uncover a mask that he had worn for a very long time. As we explored, Jake began to identify a dissonance within himself. I asked Jake, "What would it feel like to wear something that isn't your look?" He pondered why he was so invested in his look and said, "It just wouldn't be me." As I probed deeper, Jake began to realize that looking cool was a mask he wore to cover an earlier wound.

Jake told of a childhood in which he felt feminized by his overly protective mother. She dressed him in very girlish outfits. He recalled early photos of himself in which he felt embarrassed about how he looked. Jake had been a very docile, obedient child and was rewarded for acting properly. All of this left him with a core inadequacy with regard to issues about his masculinity. So Jake began to create a mask for himself.

As he moved from adolescence into adulthood, he created the mask of a cool, rebellious man, which was in fact, the opposite of how he really felt. He was compensating for his deficit. Eventually Jake came to see that he had created a personality for himself that would defend against his insecurities. And this mask greatly affected his relationships with women. His lovers often complained about Jake's inability to be soft or nurturing.

The shoes provided Jake with an opportunity to examine who he really was beneath his mask. He came to consider what it might feel like to just be, without the encumbrance of the mask. By doing so Jake would be free to be Jake. So it seems that the simple issue of choosing shoes opened Jake up to a greater self-examination. As he unmasked, Jake developed a greater comfort with his authentic unmasked self, which brought him into more intimate relations with others.

SELF-ESTEEM OR OTHER-ESTEEM

We create our masks in an attempt to bolster our self-esteem. Yet the very term self-esteem requires scrutiny, for it is actually a misnomer. Self implies that the esteem comes from within. But when we take a closer look, it would appear that one's self-esteem is actually derived from external sources.

Ask someone what boosts their self-esteem. A student might answer good grades; a businessperson responds about their performance or a job well done. Most people feel that praise or recognition augments their self-esteem.

Generally, people believe their self-worth depends upon external approval. Although recognition from others feels good, this is not esteem that emanates from oneself. Since the esteem is derived from the outside, we can see how we modify our personalities in order to derive more external praise. In short, we create masks to get more externally derived esteem.

Admittedly, being loved or valued by others feels good, but if these external markers are removed, how do we feel about ourselves? If a mediocre performance, a criticism or lack of praise diminishes how we feel, then it becomes clear that the esteem is not self, but actually other-esteem. Self-esteem cannot be eradicated by the actions of others.

Genuine self-esteem comes from our innate sense of self, at our core. Self-esteem is authentic; it emanates from within. It is more a state of being than doing. If we remove our careers, the myriad roles that we play, our possessions and our social status, we are left with ourselves. How does that feel? Do we like, respect and love ourselves without these external markers?

We create masks to derive other-esteem. We must unmask to create the opportunity for genuine self-esteem. Unmasking is the process of developing intimacy within ourselves, thereby creating the foundation for authentic self-esteem. Without proper esteem of one's self, all relationship will be tainted by a neediness that will ultimately be projected onto one's partner.

In such circumstances we are manipulating the true self in order to derive esteem from others. Not only is this a very disempowering experience, it also sabotages relationship. It's as though we are taking our well-being and serving it on a plate to our partner. It is the other who will then decide if we are worthy. We think that we see ourselves as others see us. In truth, it is not as they see us, but rather as we think they see us. This is obviously not a healthy place to be. We must never judge ourselves on how others judge us. In fact, we should never be theirs to judge.

It is quite ordinary for people to have opinions about other people. There is a tendency, however, for us to elevate their opinions to the status of judgments. In fact, others can only render judgments when we grant them the power to judge us. If we are in a healthy and loving relationship with our inner self, we can easily tolerate other people's opinions without conferring them the status of judge.

Diane and her husband Ron had been married for twelve years.

Ron complained that he had never really been in love with Diane and that he was missing a deep and fulfilling connection. Ron openly belittled his wife, blaming her for his discontent. He felt that there was more to life and, although he and Diane shared an amicable relationship, he proposed a trial separation so that he might experience life on his own.

Diane was a rather affable woman with a quick smile, yet she lacked confidence and had a nervous laugh. She lived her life in futile attempts to please her husband, trying to maintain a veil of happiness. In fact, some years earlier when Ron told her of an affair that he had just concluded, she permitted herself only a short episode of anger before suppressing her outrage. Almost immediately she strove to become an even more dutiful wife, feeling that she must have been inadequate to cause Ron to stray.

At first, Diane was terrified at the thought of separation, but in time came to recognize her own unhappiness with her marriage. She eventually acknowledged that she deserved better. Within weeks after separating, Diane began to flower. The meek, selfless woman I had known began to transform into an empowered person in quest of her own well-being. Diane had made a commitment to finding and living her truth.

Diane joined an intimacy group that I was facilitating and was an eager learner. We spent several weeks exploring the topic of other-esteem. Before long, she reconnected with an old college flame named Tom and she proclaimed that she was falling in love with him. Diane said that he was very attentive and kind to her, and confided that she felt wonderful in his presence. Diane had never experienced such adulation. Her only concern was that Tom appeared rather amorphous. It seemed that he would do anything to please her, a behavior that she recognized all too well in herself.

In a session some weeks later, Diane said that she felt confused. She had just spent some time with Tom and although he treated her as lovingly as ever, she was concerned that her feelings for him had diminished. There now seemed to be an imbalance in their relationship. She was worried that Tom's affection for her exceeded her love for him. As we explored this more deeply, Diane discovered her deeper truth. She realized that she had been so deprived of nurturing and affection in her marriage that she had filled herself up with Tom's lavish attention.

It was Tom, not herself, who was making her feel good. She had been running on empty for so long that she had filled herself up with other-esteem. Tom provided her with a shortcut; he made her feel better. Although this may sound entirely wonderful, it should not be confused with love. Diane realized very early on that Tom was providing her with other-esteem. If she were truly in love with him, she would have had no issue of mutuality of feelings.

Diane had been unconsciously using Tom to provide herself with what she longed for. Once she became aware of this, Diane was able to honestly communicate this shift in feelings with Tom and they redirected their expectations toward a more appropriate friendship. Diane realized that she needed to develop her own esteem before she could really determine her loving feelings for another. Without her enlightenment about issues of esteem, this relationship would likely have resembled a traditional saga of falling in and out of love. Genuine self-esteem enables us to choose partners from an energy rooted in loving consciousness rather than the need basis of other-esteem.

Esteem must be created internally and can then radiate outward. If we are focused externally in our need for esteem, we are looking in the wrong place. And in so doing, we are altering our being in a purposeless manner, for all such attempts at happiness are superficial and futile.

Let's consider what happens when we first begin the dating process. We put our best foot forward so that the other person will think more highly of us. Is it our true self we are presenting, or a masked version to induce the other to like us? We are on our best behavior so that we may generate the desired response. Of course this entire dance of intimacy becomes pointless given that eventually our true self will emerge. So, in fact, we are setting ourselves up for future disappointment.

We are manipulating the interaction so that the other person likes and approves of us. But it is not the true self that is presented. We are arranging for them to like who we pretend to be, not who we are. It's not that endearment and romance must fade, we're simply creating that outcome by our deceptions. Too often, we are falling in love with someone's false personality, not their true essence. And so we speak of falling out of love. It might be more appropriate to consider that we didn't truly know one another from the start.

Let's take another look at masks and their relation to self-esteem. Karen entered therapy presenting complaints about her marriage. Karen and Jim had been married for twenty years, and although there was an absence of conflict, there was an absence of joy as well. Karen and Jim lived the form of the marriage, but the inner content was absent. Although Jim seemed satisfied to live this way, Karen's turmoil festered just beneath the surface. Karen's jocular appearance belied her frustration with her life as she struggled to truly assert herself.

After a few introductory sessions we began to explore Karen's childhood. She told of a mother given to periodic bursts of rage and an alcoholic father. As a child Karen created a personality role for herself as peacemaker. She would avoid her mother's anger by placating her and trying to soothe the turbulence of her troubled family. Karen didn't have the safe haven that children deserve, so she adjusted her personality in an attempt to manipulate her mother's behavior and lessen its impact. By doing this she was able to better preserve a safe place for herself. So Karen began to wear the mask of being a people-pleaser. Her self-esteem was deficient due to the fact that her parents were unavailable to her in any reasonable manner. Karen created a protective shell of other-esteem by trying to please others. Of course, Karen lost her own true identity in the process.

As an adult, Karen expended much energy in avoiding stressful confrontations. This was no surprise in light of her childhood. Her marriage was greatly affected by this tendency. Rather than engage her husband in areas that might be upsetting or create disharmony,

Karen's tendency was to sweep things under the rug. With her friends she went to great lengths to distance herself from discord. She turned much of her attention toward her daughter, to whom she was unusually close. All of these behaviors produced a passivity in Karen that sabotaged her ability to enjoy intimate relationships with others. Her people-pleaser mask inhibited Karen's capacity for authentic interactions. She turned her frustrations and anger inward to avoid unpleasantness with others.

In one session Karen shared a dream with me. In her dream her mother was yelling at her, and Karen was playing the role that she had come to know so well. She was both avoiding and placating her mother. As we analyzed this dream, it emerged that what appeared to be her mother's anger was really Karen's. Often, our dreams present other people who are merely actors representing different parts of our own self. Karen identified that the part being played by her mother was really Karen. In this circumstance, Karen was angry with herself for not being able to engage in adult relationships in a meaningful way. Her unconscious sent her the message via her dream that she needed to find her true self. The personality she had created was the result of seeking approval from others. She began to see that the mask she wore was getting in her way. It no longer suited her. The message came to Karen through her dream and she was now ready to begin unmasking.

As the process of unmasking unfolded, Karen's marriage to Jim came to life as she was now empowered to face difficult situations. She no longer hid from truth or unpleasantness. Karen's personality shifted from people-pleaser and she began to develop a new self-identity. Karen certainly encountered some fear as she shed her old mask, but the rewards were well worth it.

We can see from these examples that we can not have intimate relations with others before we have them with ourselves. Unmasking is a continual process. It is a lifetime journey, but once undertaken, this quest can help anyone move toward their highest self and open to intimate relations with others.

Once during a talk I was giving a man in the audience asked, "If you can feel so wonderful about yourself, then what's the purpose of relationship with another?" I pondered this for a moment and answered, "Imagine yourself listening to the most rapturous music, with your eyes closed, gently moving to the rhythm. Everything is perfect in the moment. All is well in your relationship with yourself. You are in need of nothing. What could be better? Now open your eyes and see a lover enfolded in your arms, sharing the dance with you. Your lover didn't join you because of your need, but their presence makes a delightful relationship (with yourself) even more spectacular. That is the vision of another enhancing your life."

In the best-selling book *Conversations with God* we are told, "The purpose of relationship is not to have another who might complete you; but to have another with whom you might share your completeness." This thought underscores the necessity of unmasking in order to reach our true selves. If we move toward our own wholeness, we are no longer entering into relations with our partners from a place of neediness. Instead, we are committed to integrating our shadow and completing our moon.

Sometimes people become concerned that the more self-aware they become, the more difficult it might be to find their future mate. They ask if they are becoming too particular or selective. How will they ever find the right partners if so many are now the wrong choice?

The more deeply you know yourself, the greater your shadow has been integrated, the more conscious you have become, and the clearer your focus is on choosing appropriate partners. And the field of potential partners will certainly be narrowed. But that is exactly as it should be. For having selected a love partner by means of a process that focuses on conscious and authentic motivation, you will ultimately increase the likelihood of joy and fulfillment in your relationship. Rather than choosing from an array of unlimited lovers, this awakening will provide an opportunity to harmonize with those with who are most appropriate for us. This consciousness enables us to open to our soul partners. This is a vital step in the journey of our souls.

Chapter 4

RELATIONSHIP AND LOVE

It is our soul's purpose to explore, to experience, and to expand.

REJECTION

We often create our masks to protect us from rejection. By altering our personalities and fencing with intimacy, we are actually putting our energy into little more than avoiding rejection. So great does the fear of rejection become that we may wall ourselves off from potential lovers. Thus, the mere threat of rejection is enough to block intimacy and, paradoxically, induces behavior that will likely preclude intimacy. If we have closed ourselves off from intimacy, we are all but ensuring emotional isolation. We have, essentially, blocked ourselves from authentic interaction with others.

The irony is that another person doesn't really have the power to reject you. For you were never theirs to reject. One of the great pains of life may come from the sorrow caused by a departed lover. You may feel as though your heart has been ripped from your chest. You may anguish that part of yourself which is gone forever. The enormity of this despair may plunge anyone into depression. How could he do this to me, you might ask? It may feel like the ultimate rejection. The unique energy that you shared and the wonderful experiences may now be relegated to memories. And this is, indeed, a poignant loss; however, it is not rejection.

The sense of rejection is really due to a lack of self-love. For whatever reasons, the other person made a choice in life and decided to end the relationship. It was their choice about their life. It reflects on them as much as you. Of course, if you joined with that person in an attempt to complete yourself, you will undoubtedly see their behavior as rejection. Their departure represents a rejection of the self that needed them in order to attain your own completion.

If we loved ourselves sufficiently from the start and selected the other from choice rather than need, the entire concept of rejection would shift. We choose to be with another and we may come to decide to no longer be with them. Life is an endless sequence of choices. In our suffering we may select to internalize another's life choice as our rejection, but in truth, it is not. Rather than dwelling on the loss of our partner and its incumbent feelings of rejection, it is far more useful to contemplate the original loss of love in our life. It is our childhood loss of self-love that creates the very notion of rejection.

In fact, it is this original rejection of self that compels us to seek love and approval from others. As soon as we adorned our masks we betrayed ourselves in an attempt to make it all right through the approval of others. Essentially, what we do is deny our own rejection of self and unknowingly confer upon others responsibility for our well-being. We make them responsible for our happiness. It's as if we are saying, "go ahead, make me okay for me." If we are making someone else responsible for our happiness, we have surrendered our power. This is a prescription for unhappiness and blame.

It's easier to blame them than to accept our responsibility. Our lack of self-esteem is really our rejection of self. For if we love ourselves, we cannot be rejected. Relationship with one's self must precede relationship with others. You can't genuinely love or be loved by another until you love yourself. There are no exceptions. You may care for another, be dependent upon them for your own sense of love, but that is not to be confused with unselfish love.

For love to be unselfish, it must be without need. Only then can we honestly love the other without expectations of reciprocity. We must experience our own self-love in an appropriate manner, thereby eliminating the need to extract love from the other. We are then free to experience the true energy of love. A love relationship that flows from authentic and empowered choice is a gift that transforms the mundane into a sacred experience.

CONDITIONAL LOVE

We are coming to see that we seek love in a very circuitous manner. We love another so that they may in turn love us and give us what we could not provide for ourselves to begin with. Clearly, this is unconsciously manipulative and somewhat fear-oriented behavior. A relationship based upon this premise, as most are, is controlling.

The drama usually unfolds this way: I'll love you as long as you love me, but if you stop loving me I'll be angry and I won't love you any longer. This phenomenon doesn't appear particularly loving. Yet this is typical. Most relationships are not based upon the deeper nature of love. Love has no conditions. It simply is. Love between two people is an energy that resonates in a profound manner. Love energy does not speak the language of conditions, expectations or rules.

Sadly, most of us don't come to experience such love—and our relationships suffer for it. Usually we enter into relationships from a needy place, so we are not yet ready to experience unconditional love. From this perspective, many people often reflect that they have never truly been in love. Although we readily employ the word love, we practice it in a very adulterated form. And so we speak of falling in and out of love when we are really falling in and out of need. Authentic love cannot be experienced in a fear-based relationship. Love flourishes only in the absence of fear.

The fear of your partner no longer loving you may predominate the energy of the relationship. If he or she no longer loves you, you may feel you are no longer worthy of love. Again, this is because you don't have sufficient love for yourself. Therefore, many people will manipulate their relationship for the purpose of keeping the other in line. A perceived loss of love may become preferable to having your partner actually leave the union, for that leaves you alone. And clearly unloved. If you can maintain the status quo, you may rationalize your unhappiness by blaming your partner. Behavior based upon this premise serves as a primary ingredient for failure in relationship.

Control is not loving; it is fear-based. It does not permit each to see the other as unique, sacred and ever changing. The tendency may be to restrict the other's behavior to insure the false security of the status quo. One of the means by which we control our partners is by selecting which thoughts we will share with them. We behave in this manner in an attempt to control their reactions. We might fear the consequences of sharing the truth and so we create relationships that fail to grow and thrive. We come to think of the relationship in terms of ownership, as if we have a deed to our partner. Lovers are not possessions. Love in these circumstances is not at all what we might have imagined. This is when we may come to say that we love our partner but that we're not in love with them. Often this is a result of our fear-based constraints that impinge upon the love energy.

The purpose of relationship is, of course, multi-faceted. A fundamental reason for relationship is to serve as a vehicle for our growth and spiritual evolution. By joining with another in intimacy, we may come to know more deeply of ourselves. The loving partnership may then foster a deeper revelation of the self.

Yet, ordinary relationship blocks that process from the fear that if our partner changes, then we may be alone. Too often, this kind of relationship impinges upon one's spiritual evolution and the self becomes lost in the relationship. So a fundamental dilemma arises; are we to remain in the false security blanket that the form of a relationship provides or are we to utilize the relationship to help us grow toward our full potential? The paradox really suggests that the most expedient way to maintain your relationship and benefit from it might be to loosen the ties that bind.

Picture a couple floating down the stream of life together, hand in hand. They enjoy many experiences together and their partnership serves them well. They find comfort sharing their life's journey together until one day they see an island ahead of them in the stream. One wants to travel to the left side, the other to the right. Each is seeking a different experience. If each insists upon taking their route, conflict and hostility usually erupts. If they cannot agree and don't let go of one another's hand, they may crash into the island, signifying the end of the relationship. Yet, if they lovingly release their grip on one another, they might well rejoin after they have passed the island. This suggests a more spiritual relationship that is not based upon fear or control. This depiction illustrates that the nature of conscious relationship must redirect its energy toward growth and exploration, not control.

THE MISTAKE

Our beliefs about concepts such as mistakes and failure often prevent us from moving into deeper, more rewarding experiences of life. I believe that there is no such thing as a mistake. Relationship creates the opportunity for new experience. Yet, the avoidance of pain and sadness often limits our ability to experience what we must. These struggles are often necessary to propel us toward deeper truth and cognition in our evolution. The concept of failure comes from a nomenclature of fear and is an artificial construct of our belief in the reality of mistakes.

The fear of making a mistake paralyzes people. Yet, what is a mistake? Generally, a mistake is seen to be a decision that we may come to regret. Most people try to avoid what we refer to as mistakes because they cause pain. Ironically, the pain that we attempt to avoid may be exactly what we need to experience. The marriage that turned bad and was ultimately severed by divorce may be seen through the prism of having been a mistake. However, without that experience neither party may have had the opportunity to uncover greater truths about themselves and to learn from the experience to move on to greater joy. These reflections and insights about our partners and ourselves are intrinsic to our spiritual path. They are an essential part of our learning.

When we are terrorized by the thought of making mistakes, we lose the opportunity to experience life more fully. There is never a single correct decision or solution. The more we participate with and fully engage in life's exploration, the more spontaneity and playfulness emerge. And the more potential for joy appears. Wonder and awe reappear. These are the building blocks of a loving relationship and a fulfilling life.

SYNCHRONICITY

There is a synchronicity to life that does not include the construct of mistakes. Carl Jung, who originated the word, defines synchronicity as "...a meaningful coincidence of two or more events, where something other than the probability of chance is involved." His insight was that events that appear to have no meaningful connection are in fact, completely interrelated. The more we open to our intuition and release thoughts about mistakes, the more we are in harmony with our higher purpose. Instead of struggling to resist the changes of life, it's as if we are letting the universe take over and guide us. There is a natural unfolding to our lives if we just permit it to happen.

Concepts such as mistake, failure and rejection block us from the richness of our life's journey. Synchronicity implies a magical tapestry of love and purpose. The more we open to the flow of life, the more we experience these amazing coincidences. And we come to see that they are not coincidences at all, only the actualization of our being.

A number of years ago I was engaged in an entirely different vocation. I ran a business that provided me with a rewarding income, but lacked in fulfillment and passion. After several successful years the business experienced a downturn and I was forced to close the operation. At the time I may have looked upon my business decisions ruefully, regretting the mistakes that I had made. Yet those decisions, which resulted in upheaval and loss at that time, opened another door for me. Those so-called "mistakes" permitted me to find my soul's work. As one door closed another opened.

We may not immediately recognize that new door, as we focus on our fears of the unknown. However, the absence of comfort should never be construed as a mistake. The new portals that we venture through provide us with infinite opportunities. To benefit from them, all we need is a shift in perspective.

It is our soul's purpose to explore, to experience, and to expand. Relationship provides a vehicle for this. It is said that life is a journey; however, a journey means not knowing the destination. There is no roadmap for this journey because when we look ahead at the destination, we miss the opportunities that open to us along the way. If our gaze is always focused ahead, at the result, we will miss the experience of the moment, and again we find ourselves sleepwalking through life. Ask yourself, "Is my life an exploration? Am I exhilarated at the unknown opportunities for new experiences and do I view my relationship as a vehicle for the expansion of my soul?" If so, you do not honor the word mistake. On the other hand, if this question made your eyebrows arch in disbelief, some deeper self-reflection might be helpful. For you are likely living a life tempered by fear.

Our belief in synchronicity opens us to trusting our intuition. Dreams are a powerful transmitter of these messages, embedded within in the depths of our unconscious. During our sleep, when our personality and ego have receded, our dreams convey information that it intends for us to utilize. This is a manner in which our soul communicates with us, free of the conditioned bias of the personality.

Earlier in my career as a psychotherapist, I had gravitated toward working with men. In fact, I was facilitating a group for men, and was considering practicing exclusively with men. I was laboring with this decision until a dream emerged. In this dream I was playing baseball in a schoolyard. The field resembled the childhood playground that I had played upon and was made of concrete. I much preferred playing on grass and I suggested to the other players that we travel to another field some distance away. They agreed and we found ourselves on a beautiful grass baseball field. However, we found ourselves suddenly short of players, so I wandered off in search of some additional ballplayers. I somehow found myself outside of an aerobic class full of women, whereupon I entered and asked if any of the women would like to join our ballgame. A number of them did, and we went off and had a glorious game of baseball on a magnificent field.

I interpreted the dream in the following manner: First, if I wanted to realize my career vision, I would have to be prepared to leave the "concrete" to play on the field of my dreams. Just as important, I would need the energy of women to make this vision come to life. My dream had guided me toward my path. Women are now a very important part of my work and I am most grateful that I followed the synchronous message of my dream.

The powerful fear and threat of mistake imprisons us. Who is to judge as to what is a mistake? Who decides? The very notion of mistake elicits a constrictive reaction that suggests conformity and fear. We dishonor our intuition, our hearts and our curiosity when we mesh with the gears of the automaton that directs our "proper" behavior. In this state we hear only the voices of others, voices that tell us how to act but never ask us how we feel. When your own inner voice cries out in alarm and warns you not to make a mistake, respond gently, "it's alright, there is no such thing." I came upon a plaque once that read, "A mistake is an event, the full benefit of which has not yet been turned to your advantage." The fear of mistakes shackles our relationships, curtails our learning and growth, and deprives us of the three E's, exploration, experience, and expansion. The choice is simple. Are we to live our lives directed by the voices of others or are we to find our inner voice and create life through our own experience?

THE RULES

If a primary purpose of relationship is to come to know more deeply of yourself, then an ancillary reason is to experience joy and fulfillment. Relationship is not designed to be a duty or replete with obligation. Yet we live as though these rules exist. There is an implicit belief that one must honor the form of the relationship, even at cost of self-effacement. Guilt and obligation are cultural imperatives that we have affixed to relationship in a neurotic compulsion to deprive ourselves of happiness. These dictates again honor the form of the relationship, but entirely dishonor the content.

In a therapy session with Paul, a reticent man in his mid-thirties, the conversation turned to his image of a perfect life. His ideal was already complete, at least in its form: an attractive wife, two children, a very successful medical practice and a beautiful house. He had it all. Yet the more he clung tenaciously to his myth of happiness, the more miserable he was. He and his wife hadn't had sex in nearly two years and shared little emotionally. He was frustrated that his life was empty, but a resounding voice kept telling him that he had no right to complain. He asked himself, "Don't I have a responsibility to maintain the guise of a happy life?"

Paul was confronting his myth. We discussed his concerns with selfishness. I told him that it was indeed selfish if he had no sense of self to share. If he was unhappy and unable to nurture himself appropriately, what was it that he had to offer others? Nurturing one's self is the most unselfish thing one can do. If your tank is always running low, you have little to give.

Not taking care of yourself is selfish. Again we are confronted with a paradox. To be truly unselfish you must first provide for your inner self. Fill yourself up with reverence and self-respect and you have much to offer the world. Self-denial has no intrinsic worth and limits your fullness, thereby restricting what you have to offer another.

Relationship should serve as a vehicle for joy. If we honor the innate values of pleasure and enchantment, rather than the societal lip service to the form of the relationship, our lives might well flourish. There are those who protest that it is irresponsible or wrong to terminate a relationship just because we are unhappy. I respond, "Who says so? Who made the rules?" It is our purpose to be happy. Obviously, I am not suggesting that we leave relationships on a whim; however, with honest exploration and self-examination, we may come to a better understanding of whether the relationship serves our highest purpose. This self-reflection should clarify our own responsibility regarding the state of our relationship and happiness.

Clearly, the rules by which we relate are not serving us. Indeed, this code of behavior demonstrates a penchant for masochism. The contradiction between the earlier hopes for happiness and the later resignation into mediocrity is a script for crazy making. First we believe that we will find happiness by virtue of a long standing relationship. When we don't, for a multitude of reasons, an epic force informs us that responsibility and duty to the status quo are the moral directives of a proper life. This resignation must be confronted if we are to provide ourselves with the love that we deserve. It is time to send this rulebook back from whence it originated and rewrite the rules. The new rules of relationship must be founded upon commitment to intimacy, passion, wonder and fulfillment.

Chapter 5

REWRITING THE RULES

OF RELATIONSHIP

Let us not follow where the path may lead,
let us go instead where there is no path... And leave a trail.
— *A Japanese Proverb*

As we are coming to see, our lack of self-exploration contributes to the malaise of our relationships. Yet, the very system of relationship needs deeper examination. When so many suffer in their relationships, attention must be focused upon the system that produces these results. Systems theorists tell us that we must look beyond the individual to the structure that shapes the individual's reality. Clearly, the system of relationship that we encounter is producing abysmal results.

The rules of relationship must be rewritten so that they honor the content, not simply the form. To enter into partnerships that play by old rules that ensure failure is simply unconscious. If we are to make intimate relationship our priority, it would make sense to consciously create a method of relating that honors relationship as sacred.

We need to learn how to be present and communicate in different ways, how to share the truth without fear of consequences, how to get past boredom and recreate wonder and passion in our lives. In other words, we have to rewrite the script of our relationships and our lives.

IN THE MOMENT

Can you recall what it was like when you first fell in love? Do you remember the experience of spending hours together, just sitting and talking, with maybe some hugging and kissing thrown in? At the end of that time together you may have looked at your watch in disbelief. How could that have possibly been two hours, you asked yourself? It felt more like twenty minutes. Why did the passage of time seem so different? Because you were really there, present in every way. Both of you were eager to learn about one another and to share every thought. Since you had little history together, you weren't thinking of the past. And the future certainly wasn't predictable yet. So you were attentive in the present moment. You probably noted your partner's every nuance. If you think back, you might even recall some particulars, the clothes you wore, the setting or perhaps the fragrances in the air. Many such details may linger in your memory. These pictures remain because you were present. You were not sleepwalking through the event.

Time seemed to fly because you were consciously present in the moment. One result was that the moment was probably full of enchantment and awe, and that's what love feels like. And that is precisely what makes us feel most alive.

To experience love you must be present in the moment. Wonder is also a vital ingredient in this formation of love energy. But again, wonder, enchantment and awe are only possible when we are present. Only then is there a harmony between intellect and spirit. We are feeling as much as we are thinking. The rational mind is not yet controlling our experience and our heart is fully participating. The soul is completely present and we are at peace with our being. The ecstasy may feel like finally being home. It's a return to our source. Now the relationship is reflecting our most genuine state. This is what people typically refer to as "falling in love". Yet, this state of bliss fades all too soon.

THE RERUN

Unfortunately, there is a tendency in relationships to start to play old reruns in our heads. I have witnessed many an exchange between couples when it seemed that neither party was really there. For example, two people are involved in a disagreement. As they are arguing, one says, "You said that!" In disbelief their partner fires back, "What do you mean? I never said anything like that!"

After you see these exchanges a few times, you have to wonder who these people were talking to; obviously not one another. They didn't even hear each other so they can't possibly agree on what was said. In effect, no one was present. Why is that?

The reason is that we are usually not listening. Instead, we are playing an old rerun in our minds. We think we know only too well what's coming out of the other's mouth, and we're busily preparing our response. We don't even hear a word. We are not present. We have our truth and they have theirs. We can never hear the other's truth when we're so preoccupied defending our own. Instead of listening carefully to what the other person is saying, we are off thinking about the best argument to convince them that they're wrong and we're right. It's hardly surprising that neither is connecting. The relationship now resembles a debating club, not an exercise in loving intimacy. Since we are caught up in the mental drama of our script, our hearts are no longer open. Rather than fostering understanding and compassion, such exchanges deplete the love energy.

The insidious habit of absenting the self and becoming deaf to meaningful communication causes boredom, loss of love and a host of other problems that sabotage the relationship. Let's look a little further into the implications of not being present.

Our memory banks are full of past interactions. It is important to realize that these are not the events themselves, only current perceptions of past events. As time goes by there is a tendency to shape the memory to fit our current belief about our partners and ourselves. This is why two people end up with very different memories of past interactions. If one person has lost touch with loving feelings for the other, their recollection of past events will be filtered to support their current feelings.

I recently worked with a couple who were obviously experiencing the death throes of their marriage. He no longer felt love for his wife of twelve years and his memories of their relationship were focused upon the negative interactions. He had come to see her as an adversary, which was consistent with his loss of affection for her. She thought she was still in love with her husband and was honestly bewildered by his different recollections of their past. She recalled an essentially loving relationship. Since she still loved him and was committed to saving the marriage, her perceptions of the past were equally filtered by the needs of her current emotional state.

Inevitably, they would waste their time arguing about who was right or wrong about their memories of the marriage. If only they could accept that their thoughts were being shaped by their current needs and expectations, they might disengage from fruitless argument and turn to more important issues. The real concern should be about sharing their truths in the present, detached from the argument of past events.

Once we come to know one another well, there is a tendency to assume how the other thinks and acts. So we edit a memory of them and project it into the future. Thus, our current perception of the past actually becomes the future. Having now created the future out of our past belief system, we have locked ourselves into a box. And we can no longer find the way out. When we perceive things out of a habitual response born of the past, we limit the future to the same behaviors and are never there in the present moment.

Let's look at what happens when we are not in the present. For one thing we stop learning. Anything new that our partner has to offer is deflected and relegated to the known niche that our memory bank has placed them in. When you stop learning, the vitality of the relationship withers. You grow bored and lose interest in the other person. After all, you assume you automatically know everything there is to know about the other person. So the relationship becomes stagnant. You look for reasons to avoid your partner. You may occupy yourself with other things or other people. Or you may become frustrated, sparking conflict. Under these circumstances there is a greater likelihood that you will act out your frustrations. Now what do you suppose happens to your intimacy and sex life?

In any given moment there are infinite possibilities. Opening to the spontaneity of the moment, being fully alive, free from the constraints of the old rerun opens us to limitless possibilities. Let's go back to when we first met our lover. No memory banks were operating yet, so we had to listen attentively. In fact, we wanted to listen. It was fascinating. So what happened? The original object of your desire is still the same person. What changed?

Most likely, you both went to sleep. The old script played on until both of you felt your buttons fully triggered. Nobody elected to be attentive and present and so your future was already decided upon.

What's required is to awaken and once more come alive to the moment. When our relationships are based upon predictive assumptions and we know the outcome in advance, there is no chance that things will turn out differently. Because we are writing the script for that outcome, the future is already ascertained. That being the case there isn't any need to be present. No wonder we fall out of love so easily. It's not that love and passion have to die. It's just that we are living and behaving in a manner that will cause that to occur. Each decision or feeling at a particular moment can create a new energy in your relationship which begins at that moment and extends outward from that point.

THE SPIDER'S WEB

When we sleepwalk through life, inattentive and unconscious, we think of our lives as a straight line from past to present to future. As we have seen, these linear demarcations all blur into one reality. So the past becomes the present, and if there is no change of perspective, it will also become the future. One way to break out of this imprisoning way of seeing is to imagine yourself in the middle of a spider's web. There is no past in this web, just a starting point in the center. All around you in every direction are an infinite number of pathways. All are open to you. You are free to choose one, then another. You are not constrained by the mental and emotional baggage of your past. In fact, there is no past; all that exists is the moment that you are in and every new moment creates a new time-line of reality.

In the more common, linear picture of time, our image of the past actually creates the future. But remember this is not a limitless future, it's already been decided. In a way, it's almost as though we are living time backwards. Our memory of the past becomes the present, so in fact, we have no present.

Using the spider web visualization, in the center of the web, there is no past. You have freed yourself from that illusion. All paths open. Each choice you make creates a new time-line. If you feel frozen by the vast alternative of choices, just recall that there is no such thing as a mistake. And as you choose a direction, you are always free to choose yet another, since the choices are indeed infinite. The same can be true of your relationship experience. When you become present in the moment you can consciously choose a new script for your relationship.

TIME

*Time must never be thought of as pre-existing in
any sense; it is of a manufactured quantity.*
—Hermann Bondi

So said Bondi, the famous British mathematician and cosmologist, and indeed a brief consideration of the concept of time may be helpful in shifting paradigms about our personal sense of reality. Albert Einstein certainly shattered the notion of the machine-like quality of time with his revelation of relativity. We now accept, at least intellectually, that time is relative. A minute on the Moon elapses differently than a minute on Earth. An astronaut traveling at super warp speeds would return to earth far less aged than the contemporaries he left behind. In spite of these astounding discoveries, we still adhere to many myths about time which, in turn, limit the actualization of our consciousness.

In his book, *The Fabric of Reality*, David Deutsch suggests that indeed there is no passage of time. Nothing moves from one moment to the next; not even time. In other words time does not flow. He states that what we experience is "The difference between our present perceptions and our present memories of past perceptions." He says that it is incorrect to conclude that our consciousness, or anything for that matter, moves through time.

Deutsch continues by explaining that we are aware of events that we experience. And each experience results in a state of consciousness that we attach to it. That consciousness does not move forward in time. Yesterday's consciousness belongs to yesterday. If we choose a similar consciousness for today, it becomes today's. The actual events may lie in yesterday, today or tomorrow. One may precede the other; however, they are different events, with different states of consciousness and memory. The notion that time really flows is more a metaphor than a reality.

> *The distinction between past, present and future*
> *is only an illusion, albeit a stubborn one.*
> *—Albert Einstein*

These insights help us to see that if we shift our perception of time flowing along some kind of line, we may free ourselves to see that what we experience is a collection of snapshots of life's events. As life proceeds we have an ever-increasing portfolio of snapshots. This departure from the traditional way of comprehending time permits us to unburden ourselves from the baggage of our past. The past to which we refer is simply a collection of pictures of events already experienced. For the sake of illustration, let's estimate that we will experience approximately two and one-half billion seconds in the average seventy-year life. There is no mandate that they all more or less resemble one another. So if we have already lived one and one half billion of those seconds, we can now select differently for those yet unrealized.

There is no innate predilection to continue the same succession of experiences; we are free to take new snapshots at any moment that we choose. But if we continue to select old pictures that portray negativity or mediocrity, then we are generating brand new snapshots that replicate the old ones.

This shift in consciousness liberates us to choose differently in the next moment. And this is an essential insight for enabling us to awaken to the moment, unencumbered by the baggage that we think we carry with us. We can release the baggage the instant we select a new snapshot to experience. The past needn't imprison us; our current perceptions of the past are our excuses for carrying our past into the future.

DIALOGUE

As you are engaged in conversation with your partner, ask yourself, where are my thoughts right now? We each carry our own belief system. And it is that mental map that usually convinces us that we are have' truth than our partner does. Our individual belief system is our unique way of seeing the world and the people in it. It shapes our reality. Our mental model creates our reality by telling us how to perceive events and people. So as we begin to talk to one another, we cling to our belief that we have the truth or that we are right and that the other person is wrong.

So instead of authentic communication, we find ourselves trying to convince the other person that they are wrong. While we do this neither person is listening. Each has their thoughts turned inward, planning how to persuade the other to accept their point of view. So we have literally turned off to each other, in an effort to justify our behavior or thoughts. This type of exchange is known as conversation.

In such a conversation we are passionately adhered to our own belief system. Our goal is to illustrate our partner's fallacy. Our way of seeing is tightly locked into this mental model. The result is we have two people talking at one another, but really comprehending little.

Again, each party engages in defensive reasoning rather than real communication. The need to defend our beliefs and our own particular mental model prevents us from hearing our partner and from learning. And it robs the relationship of vitality. Enter boredom, the logical product of the absence of learning. We are cut off, no longer engaging the other in a present and loving manner. Compassion and intimacy cannot exist in such an environment. We remain completely stuck in the script of our past behaviors. And we are writing the plot for unhappiness.

To break through we need real dialogue. The word dialogue comes from the Greek dia logos, which means "flow of meaning." But rather than a flow of meaning, we select fragments of thoughts and words to accept or refute our partner's voice. We are talking at each other, not interacting in a meaningful manner. And always present are the unspoken underpinnings based upon the beliefs and assumptions of each party. This defensive, fragmented way of communicating precludes us from seeing the bigger picture.

In the process of dialogue each must temporarily suspend their old beliefs and enter into a new type of exchange. Dialogue permits us to play with new ideas and new concepts without deciding right or wrong, or assigning blame. This exercise is similar to the Zen Buddhist notion of beginner's mind, in which one keeps their mind in a state of eagerness for new learning. In order to actuate this learning, ingrained beliefs and assumptions must be shed so that we may empty the mind to see differently.

In fact, for relationship to thrive there must be a playful exchange that awakens the energy and permits new learning. The moment we regress to who-said-what, or become fearful of saying something stupid, or make accusations, the dialogue ends. Instantly, we are back to the habitual, mindless pattern of conversation. This is conversation in which each party is attached to their mental models that inhibit our ability to hear, to learn and to be present.

However, in meaningful dialogue we are able to observe our thoughts and come to understand how these thoughts create our reality. It is imperative in dialogue that both people agree in advance not to engage in judgments about right or wrong. For there is no need to justify anything if there is no blame. This removes us from the need to defend ourselves.

Once freed from this compulsion, we become available to listen and consider in new ways. As the genuine dialogue opens up, we wake up and start to write a brand new script. Because old communication barriers are removed, we are able to share our deeper truths. This may be hard work at first. But the process becomes easier once we remove the old inhibitions. Not unlike the process of unmasking, we must constantly delve to deeper levels to excavate the underlying truths of our lives. This unburdening can feel exhilarating as we come into truthful expression with our partner. Equally important, the process of dialogue practically eliminates argument.

THE ARGUMENT

Almost without exception arguments avoid the real issues. In fact, the crisis at hand often has little or nothing to do with the real problems that are fueling the emotions of the moment. For most people, the deeper issues are too frightening. So we deftly avoid the problem, attempting instead to diffuse our turmoil about secondary concerns. When couples argue, they have usually just chosen a safer battleground, a familiar site, to vent some frustration and come back to fight another day. But nothing changes. Everyone feels stuck and frustrated. The energy is spent putting out the fires of these skirmishes rather than addressing the underlying problems.

It is the fear of the unsettling, deeper truth that creates the diversion into argument. Liken this to a volcano, with all its tumult and agitation ever ready to erupt. Eventually the volcano hurls lava and rocks many miles from the source of the eruption. If we conclude that the brush fires witnessed off in the distance are the problem, we are being deceived. Like the distant brush fire, the argument is only a manifestation of the deeper disharmony. We must uproot the real source of the unrest. We need to look not at the event, but at the system that produced the event.

Jane and Sam had been married for about fifteen years when they came to see me. Jane was an attractive woman of thirty-five, Sam an up-and-coming Wall Street banker. Although they enjoyed a very active social life, Sam complained that Jane was over-doing it. Every available evening was booked with plans. This became a focal point of argument. He protested that he worked hard and wanted to spend some quiet time at home with his wife. Their sex life had all but vanished, and Sam knew that it wasn't going to improve if they were out all the time. He said that he was too tired to be socializing so much. Jane rebutted that she really enjoyed her nights out with her friends and didn't want to be deprived. Each accused the other of being selfish. Their fights continued.

I assisted them in creating dialogue. No right, no wrong, no blame, just sharing their deepest feelings. Once they were able to let go of issues of blame and guilt they were able to move toward the real source of their unrest.

In time, Sam admitted he was gravely concerned about their sex life and felt that his wife was avoiding him. I helped him to divulge this in a nonthreatening way to his wife so that she might take in what he was saying without trying to defend herself. Pretty soon Jane acknowledged that she was no longer attracted to her husband. In fact, she was bored with him. She needed the stimulation of others, she acknowledged. More to the point she admitted that she was going out so often in order to avoid having sex with her husband. Ordinarily, the inclination would have been to avoid these painful truths. But now, the dialogue had permitted the deeper issues to surface.

These people had been fighting about their social calendar because their core problem was too frightening. Issues of sexual attraction and boredom were so highly charged that both people had avoided addressing them. We could now work to discover what had happened to their intimacy and passion, and whether it could be revived. By providing a safer place to share their truths, they certainly had a better chance of succeeding. Obviously, if they continued to choose to engage in the safer argument, nothing could possibly change. They came to see that dialogue provides an opportunity to break out of their unconscious script and be present, awake and ready to communicate.

Right or wrong is often a focal point in relationship struggles. People often come into therapy hoping that the therapist will confirm that their partner is the culprit. In my work with couples, right from the start I explain that we will not engage in discussions of right and wrong. That approach cannot help their relationship. If the relationship isn't thriving, placing blame on one person will not help. Even if we could somehow judge concepts like right or wrong, which most of the time we can't, it would not help bring happiness. Rather than focusing on improving the system of the relationship, attention would be directed toward accusing and defending. Healing a relationship is founded upon moving into deeper vulnerability and fostering new insight. Defending one's position and attacking the other is war-like, not loving. Shifting the consciousness and the energy of the relationship must be the focus.

Anger precludes intimacy. When you're engaged in an angry exchange, reflect upon your anger. Anger is always a mask for fear. At the moment when you feel yourself losing it, take a mental time-out. Ask yourself what you're afraid of.

Search beneath the anger to find what triggered your fear; for it is here that the real source of the agitation lies. Then, instead of resuming your outburst, share what you're afraid of. The difference in response from your lover will be profound. Rather than inducing a defensive reaction, you're enlisting your partner as your ally. Similarly, when your partner gets angry with you try asking, "What did I say that caused you fear?" You may notice that it is exactly here, when we share our fears with one another, that we are being most intimate.

WOULD YOU RATHER BE RIGHT OR
WOULD YOU RATHER BE HAPPY?

I was recently conducting a session with a couple on the verge of separating. Their marriage had hit bottom, but they were fearful of addressing the subject of divorce. Neither seemed prepared to disengage from The Argument. As they moved inexorably toward their fate, the husband clung to the notion that he was right. He was tenacious. I had an image of a person in quicksand, which I shared with them. We know that if you're in quicksand and you thrash about, you'll go under more quickly. He acknowledged that point. I then said, "Your relationship is about to end and you're not addressing that. You're still clinging to this notion of right or wrong." I asked, "Would you rather be right or would you rather be happy?" By focusing on extraneous issues of right or wrong, we avoid the real concern: What do we need to do to be happy?

THE SEESAW EFFECT

I have seen couples so invested in The Argument that, even after the fight is over, they will argue about how they argued, the rules of arguing and who had the right to end the fight. As one person plays the role of the angry aggressor, their partner tends to be more conciliatory. Given time, the positions tend to reverse. This is what I call the seesaw effect.

Envision a couple on a seesaw. One is up and they are angry and upset with their partner. The accused party is in the lower position. The argument ensues. Eventually things begin to shift. The person in the up position begins to settle toward the ground. Meanwhile, their partner begins to elevate by taking on a more aggressive posture. In other words, they are taking turns venting and defending. One, then the other. Energy wasted in this manner reveals that these people need assistance in coming to terms with the bigger picture.

Until they affect a place of balance on the seesaw, they will never be able to communicate authentically. By sliding up and down, they are unconsciously playing out power positions that underscore their lack of commitment to positive change. They must disengage from their drama and shift their perspective.

Richard and Linda, in their early forties, engaged me in an attempt to help their marriage. Richard saw his wife as very emotionally abusive and neglectful. He blamed her for the entirety of his unhappiness. By the second counseling session he had decided that separation was the best route. I surmised that Richard had in fact decided upon this path prior to entering into therapy. Linda felt rejected and abandoned. She didn't share the same view of their marriage. Linda agreed that their relationship wasn't joyful, but she felt that it wasn't bad enough to warrant a separation. She couldn't accept that Richard was no longer open to marital therapy and was, in fact, leaving.

The couple did separate and I continued to work with them individually. Linda began to cope with the changes in her life, caring for her children and herself. After several months Richard began to shift his perception of Linda and he invited her back into therapy with him. Linda said she wouldn't go back into therapy with Richard until he made amends for leaving her. As you might surmise, his side of the seesaw was declining. As it did, Linda's rose. Until they both got off the seesaw, they would never be in a position to affect healthy change in their marriage.

To invoke another image that might be helpful, imagine your

partner and yourself as spokes on the same wheel. The wheel is hurtling down a steep hill and approaching the edge of a cliff. The wheel is picking up speed as you rush toward your demise. As long as you argue, it's impossible to change course. Yet, you ignore the fate that awaits you.

You both need to change the direction of the wheel. And that will not be accomplished with issues of blame. As long as we can project blame onto our partner, we needn't take our own responsibility for changing anything. And nothing will change. To improve our relationships, we must begin to learn new techniques to break out of the old recurring habits that limit us. Only then can we enjoy the pleasure and excitement of a live, creative relationship.

Again ask yourself this fundamental question: Do I want to be happy or do I want to be right? If the answer is happy, you must be ready for change. And that change must come from within. If you would rather be right, then you must realize that you're forsaking happiness. Although most people claim that they want to be happy, they are not. Unprepared for internal change and unwilling to alter stagnant thoughts and behaviors, many people opt for the status quo.

At the core of such limiting behavior is the unspoken sense that we don't deserve better. Invariably, when I ask people if they deserve to be happy, they respond affirmatively, without hesitation.

Yet their behavior precludes that happiness. Here, is a fundamental conflict. You feel that you deserve more, yet your way of being and relating leaves you short of the goal. You are confronted with a dilemma. Do I accept my plight and make the best of it or do I set about giving myself what I deserve? Regardless of what they say, most people choose to remain stuck in the known. If you really want happiness, you must commit to change.

FEAR

The exploration of new territory often induces hesitation, reluctance or fear. However understandable, our aversion to fear hinders our ability to alter our behavior. It is not surprising that most people struggle time and again with their fear as they attempt to create a better life.

Ironically, when we resist fear, it actually empowers the fear. The avoidance of the fear strengthens it. We end up expending our energy trying to repel the fear, instead of acknowledging it as a natural partner in the process of change.

Our tendency to treat fear as an outside force makes it more threatening, embodying it as an enemy. So the more that we resist, the more power we grant to our fear. This phenomenon is truly paradoxical. The very act of resistance amplifies our anxiety. In other words, that which we fear, we summon into existence. The way to end this inner warfare is to accept the fear as a necessary element of a change in consciousness. Typically, I find that fear dissipates when we let it in.

I actually advise talking to your fear. Personify it and invite it in. Say to the fear, "You're here for a reason, let me get to know you." The act of welcoming the fear integrates it within you. Once you have embraced this distressing feeling, it is no longer an external enemy. More important, you have survived that which terrified you. Once that happens, your fear will no longer hold the same power over you.

Imagine a lake in front of you, separating you from a distant shore. Let the other shore represent the vision of happiness in your life. In order to make the changes that you need, you'll have to get into the water and swim across the lake. So you gingerly walk into the lake and are somewhat repelled by the cold, dank water. It is quite uncomfortable. Nevertheless, you begin swimming toward your vision. After a few strokes you're sorely tempted to turn back. The water is quite chilly and somewhat frightening. The choice to go forward or return illustrates how we choose to deal with fear in our lives. We can return to the familiar, even if it is replete with unhappiness and pain, or we can move forward into the unknown, with its promise of fulfillment.

I recently had a discussion with a man who shared his fear of being alone. He lived alone and dealt with his fear by constantly making plans. This man attended more support groups than you could imagine. He would do anything conceivable to avoid being alone. So, the fear remained. I advised him to stop resisting his fear. He needed to spend time alone, welcome the fear and live with it. I pointed out that he was already living with what he was so terrified of, being alone. All he had to do was release his resistance to the fear and thereby lessen its powerful hold over him. The fear would no longer be an external enemy to be avoided. Once we have assimilated our fear, we are ready to welcome change into our lives.

THE WINDS OF CHANGE

Most people go to great lengths to resist or avoid change. Yet one of the most formidable barriers to joyful relationship is the conforming and restrictive tendency that emerges from the fear of change. We are comfortable with the known, even if the known is unpleasant. So we try to control our circumstances and partners to maintain the status quo.

Of course, this can never be accomplished. However indoctrinated we are in the belief that we can keep things static, it is a futile quest. And here we are confronted with yet another myth. That myth informs us that change is bad. The natural way of the universe is change. We, and all that surrounds us, are in a constant state of flux. Order is an illusion. Nothing escapes change.

Think of yourself at a much younger age. The self that you were then, though still present in many ways, is probably quite different from the self you are now. Your experiences and relationships constantly change who you are. "I'm not the same person I used to be," can be taken quite literally. The self is undergoing constant change. When we resist change, we stagnate in a state of fear. We often describe this as being "stuck."

Only when we welcome change are we on the path toward growth and transformation. Although our soul may provide us with an underlying sense of self, our actualization rides the current of change. We literally create ourselves as we go along. Embracing new insights and new ways of being in relationship is the key to enjoying intimacy and love.

Nothing in the universe resists change. So if we structure our lives to ward off change, we are trying to create an impossible and unnatural way of being. And the effort expended in this impossible task is a major cause of our unhappiness. How can we possibly flourish if we spend our lives resisting what cannot be resisted? And so we fearfully create relationships that imprison us.

All organisms thrive somewhere on the border between order and chaos. In a hurricane the large sturdy oak tree cracks, yet the flexible willow survives as it bends with the storm. The staunch resistance to the storm resulted in the demise of the powerful oak tree, yet the adaptability of the willow proved to be the real strength.

Embracing change is another way to re-envision relationship. Our relationships are alive and ever-changing. It is a false perception that they are static. If we welcome transitions rather than resist them, we can foster vitality in our lives. But if we spend our lives resisting the current–fighting to stand still–we can never enjoy the journey.

Our relationships need growth and new experiences, and new learning to stay healthy. It is absurd to think that as two young adults we agree to marry and will live out our lives together and that nothing will ever change. Unfortunately, we begin our relationships with an erroneous philosophy and restrict ourselves as a result of this misconception.

Resisting change means putting our relationship in a box to protect it from outside influences. Life may become very predictable and awfully boring in that box. Before long discontent surfaces and someone wants out.

Even so, we come to treat our relationships as possessions to be protected from new experience and change. These behaviors are motivated from fear, not love. And thus begins the death knell of the relationship.

However, if we come to accept change and, indeed welcome it, the new willingness to alter course may propel our relationships to undreamed of discoveries.

TRUTH TELLING

Intimacy can not prevail if we don't tell one another the truth. When we hide our truth from our partner, we construct a wall. Over time that wall becomes insurmountable. The accumulated frustrations and resentments form a barrier so high that neither party can surmount it.

Moreover, when we keep a part of ourselves off limits, we dishonor our partner. In effect we are saying, "Stay away. I won't let you in here." No wonder intimacy withers. Remember the reason we don't tell one another the truth is our fear of the consequences. For example, sharing the truth may cause hurt or pain. Sometimes we don't share the truth because we're afraid of being judged. Other times we just don't want to feel guilty or ashamed.

Almost without exception it is our issue with control that keeps us from sharing the truth. We are withholding thoughts or feelings from our partner because we are concerned with their reaction and the eventual outcome of sharing the truth. This fear induces controlling behavior. Typically we might justify the absence of truth telling with the rationalization that we don't want to hurt the other. This is the story that we tell ourselves. But it's just as likely that we simply don't want to face the consequences. So we manipulate our behavior in an effort to control our partner's.

Another reason for withholding our thoughts or feelings is to keep our image of ourselves intact. If our partner becomes angry or is hurt by what we have shared, we may begin to see ourselves in a different light. So by controlling how they perceive us, we can preserve the self-image that we've chosen. In other words, we can continue to wear our mask.

Clearly, the avoidance of sharing our truths in relationship is fear-based and destructive to joyful relations. And it is certainly a prescription for a lack of intimacy. For if we don't share the truth, there can be no expectation of a fulfilling love. We are actually choosing to go through life alone, albeit with a partner. A purpose of relationship is to create a safe haven for sharing our innermost being–not for selectively filtering our truths.

Dialogue, which we discussed earlier, can progress into an exercise that I call truth telling. Truth telling is a natural product of dialogue. When I work with a couple to help them move into their truth, we create the following understanding: For the length of the truth telling exercise, there is an agreement that there will be no discussion of issues of right or wrong. Furthermore, there is an understanding that at no time in the future will either person refer back to this truth telling in an accusatory or blaming manner.

This is an immensely powerful tool for freeing people to relate in an honest way. It opens everyone to listening and learning; it fosters change. By truth telling without issues of blame, we can eliminate the fear-based behavior that constricts our relationships. Without truth, the vitality of the relationship will diminish.

I was recently conducting a seminar in which a woman complained that her husband was always working. She said that he didn't care about her or the kids; he only cared about his work. His career became the over-arching complaint.

He defended himself by insisting that his family relied upon his income and declared that he had no choice in the matter. By invoking truth telling, she was able to come to her deeper issues: She didn't feel loved by her husband and, in fact, doubted whether she still loved him. These concerns were very troubling. No wonder she had been so fearful of addressing them. The consequences of discussing whether they still loved each other were very significant, so she chose the more comfortable argument about work schedules. There was less risk involved there. There was also little chance of improvement.

Truth telling enabled them to face their core problem. As I assisted them past issues of right and wrong and beyond the superficial justifications of blame, they reached a place of sufficient vulnerability to permit their truth to emerge. Now, having shared honestly with each other, we could at least focus on the love energy that was missing. As long as their conflict had revolved around peripheral issues such as work, we were unable to help them address their real problem. Truth telling enabled them to face their reality.

Truth telling is a uniquely powerful method of fostering intimacy. After all, how can we have intimacy without truth? What would we be sharing? Partial truths, hidden truths? We need to be able to share without editing, without fear. With the freedom of sharing the truth, relationship can thrive and learning and insight can proceed.

Insight comes from a momentary glimpse of seeing things differently. When we are entrenched in our beliefs, we are not open to insights. To have insight we must be able to suspend our beliefs for the moment, and listen and learn. If we continue to think as we always thought and see as we have always seen, there won't be any new insight. And without insight we are shackled to an imprisoning relationship characterized by boredom and predictability. Truth telling frees us from the constraints of a fear-based relationship.

Let's look at another example of what truth telling can do for a relationship. I was working with a couple who had been married for eighteen years. The passion had subsided somewhat for Amy and Andrew. Truth telling had helped her admit her concerns to her husband. In fact, after some encouragement, she told her husband about a man whom she had fantasized about sexually. Her confession was very painful for Andrew. But Amy's commitment to the truth permitted her to share all with her husband. This is the way it should be. These people are, after all, married. Weren't they supposed to confide in each other? Wasn't that how the relationship began?

By permitting her truth to emerge, Amy was able to process her feelings with Andrew and avoid the temptation of acting them out. In a very important way, the opportunity to share the truth created a safety valve for the release of her tension. Of course, Amy was only able to share this with Andrew because of the truth telling exercise. By understanding that her husband was not going to chastise, or rant and rave, Amy was free to be truthful. However painful this was for Andrew, they worked through this crisis together. They explored their feelings about passion in their marriage and committed to revitalizing their sex life.

If we had not established the practice of truth telling, Amy might have been more inclined to act out her fantasy by having an affair. In fact, we might well speculate that there is an inverse correlation between truth telling and infidelity. The more that we can safely share the truth, the less likely that we'll resort to secretive behaviors. The hurt that Andrew suffered is small compared to shock of betrayal from an affair. If we commit to truth and intimacy in our relationships, infinite possibilities open before us.

Hidden agendas—anything of note that we keep from our partners—obliterate intimacy and destroy healthy relationships. Our fear of criticism or judgment justifies our decision to keep such secrets, but these secrets raise the walls that separate us from our lovers and erode our love. Truth telling frees us to be open and become present in meaningful dialogue.

This is vastly different from simply re-running the habitual and unconscious scripts that fill our thought process. When we rely on the reruns, no one is present and no one is listening. Add this to the tired old conversation about right and wrong and it's a safe bet that neither person is really in the room. So preoccupied are they with preparing their responses that they have slipped into a state of mindlessness. Learning comes to a halt and either fireworks or boredom ensues. The loss of passion cannot be far behind.

The solution is truth telling. In truth telling there is no right and wrong and there is no such thing as a mistake. It is free of blame. It liberates us to listen, pay attention, be present and share our truths. The temporary suspension of our belief system frees us to really hear what the other is saying. It permits us to let go of our version of the truth. It is from this type of dialogue that insight surfaces.

Insight is the ability to perceive differently, and new insight creates new truth. This builds the foundation for a dynamic relationship that embraces growth and change. Such communication is a cornerstone for conscious relationship. It permits us to awaken and love more fully. Remember when you first met and fell in love. Dialogue was ever present. Love requires dialogue.

SHARED DEFINITION

The different meanings that we attach to our words and expressions often lead to confusion and limit our ability to communicate effectively. Most of the time we talk we assume that the things we speak of have the same meaning to everyone. But each of us attaches slightly different mental images to words and concepts. After all, a word is really only a representation of something; it's not the thing. As a map is only a representation of the territory, it's not the territory. Each word may invoke a different feeling or nuance for each person based upon his or her particular memories and experiences. If you've had the good fortune to experience a wonderful and profound love, the word love obviously brings up a different feeling than for the person who has struggled with intimacy. Yet, we usually try to communicate without truly understanding what the words mean to each of us.

We often end up in disagreements without clarifying what we're really arguing about. When we consider the word love, the confusion is abundant. One person says to the other, "I love you." Their partner responds, "Well that may be, but you're not in love with me." I assure you that every single person has their own unique interpretation of the word.

In the Greek language there are numerous words for love. Clearly, the Greeks appreciate many different nuances. Yet in our language, with only one word to covey such a complex emotion, we may argue about whether we are or aren't "in love" without ever really trying to define what we're talking about. We tend to be more concerned with the label than the meaning.

I was recently working with a couple on the issue of romance in their relationship. She had been complaining that her husband wasn't romantic enough. He had agreed to work on this problem. In their next session he enthusiastically reported that he had, in fact, been more romantic. I asked him to share what had happened and he said that he had invited his wife into bed for a back rub. As he was telling this to me somewhat proudly, I noticed his wife's eyes roll up into her head in disbelief.

They obviously had different interpretations of the word. For him, romance was physical foreplay. I asked her what she had in mind. She described emotional romance, flowers and candlelight dinners. This couple might have argued for a long time about whether he was or wasn't being romantic. But until they defined the word by identifying their different images attached to the word, they wouldn't get anywhere. Without a shared meaning they might argue incessantly, without any resolution.

That is why it's essential to ask, "What do you mean by that? What does the word mean to you?" Shared definition is an integral part of dialogue. We cannot share intimacy with one another if we don't connect with what the other is really saying. If we are simply exchanging words that have different meanings and feelings for each of us, we are talking at each other and we are not engaged in meaningful dialogue. With a better understanding of the meanings that

we attach to words, we can open to a greater intimacy with our partners. Sharing our individual and unique reflections about the different meanings of words is itself a most intimate endeavor. Merely trying this exercise gives both of you an opportunity to pause, reflect,
and engage in intimacy.

Chapter 6

PASSION

Passion is an expression of the soul's energy. It is a manifestation of unbounded love. Often passion is expressed through sexuality, but it is not limited to that form. It is an energy that takes us beyond the boundaries of the personality. When we feel passion for something or someone, we move into another state of being. We are no longer distracted by other thoughts. We are at one with our passion.

The artist immersed in creating, the lovers coupling, the surfer riding the breaking wave and the child at play all experience an altered state of consciousness. Passion diffuses boundaries and makes us one with the universe. In our ecstasy everything is perfect. We are fully centered in the moment.

Unfortunately, we have too few of these moments. We tell ourselves that we are too busy or have too many duties and obligations. We put off transcendent joys, saving them for a more convenient time. We value responsibility over passion, even though we suffer for that choice. Our lives and our relationships are denigrated by the absence of passion. We need to set new priorities that honor passion. This is a very vital element in the new paradigm for relationship.

Passion is the soul at work. In fact, when one feels passion for

one's work, there is no such thing as burnout. You may feel exhaust-
ed, but the soul engaged does not experience burnout, for when
there is passion in one's life, there is purpose. The moment is alive.

The cultural and relational obstacles to passion limit its expression. Passion flows naturally, yet becomes encumbered by the constraints that we create. In many ways children experience and exhib-
it passion more than adults. The child full of wonder or completely
engaged in play, feels passion. As adults we need to grow back into
our childhood and re-enlighten ourselves as to the essence of happiness. In fact, taking the word enlighten literally may suggest the
lightening of the load, as if to cast off the burden of too much seri-
ousness. We might well benefit from shedding some responsibility
and replacing it with some passion.

The rules of relationship within our society deprecate passion.
These rules tell us that function is worthier than feeling, form matters more than content and that doing is more important than being.
Living the correct life takes precedence over living a joyous life.
Through the externalization process discussed earlier, focusing outward, we miss the true sustenance of life. We are trained to believe
that the goals and rewards are out there somewhere. If they were,
happiness would prevail and depression would be the exception,
given the goal orientation of our culture. Obviously, we are missing
the mark. Passion emanates from within.

On more than one occasion I have counseled women who said
that they never felt any passion for their husbands. I asked them why
they married them under those circumstances. They responded that

their mothers had given them the message that passion wouldn't last anyway and that their future husbands would make good catches. The message is that the form matters more than the content and that passion is not important.

Passion is the direct result of intimacy. Intimacy with one's authentic self creates a resonance with passionate feelings. One consequence of looking outward for our fix of passion is the tendency in our culture to idolize entertainers, especially those who express unbridled passion. Frank Sinatra was an absolute and pure expression of passion. He fought his way through a song. He lived his life with the utmost passion and so we revered him for living in a manner that we are afraid to. From Elvis to Madonna, we project our own needs for passion onto these safer surrogates, so as not to upset the finely tuned balance of our technocratic lives. If Madonna or Elvis were unknowns and moved next door, we might well shun them.

They would threaten the very tenuous safety of our correct lives. Passionate demonstrations are fine, but only on stage or screen. The unspoken belief is that it is acceptable to fantasize through others, but we must suppress our own desires. Our sexual needs, often unsatisfied, are relegated to expression through substitute sources.

Pornography is a vivid example of the absence of healthy passion in our lives. People who enjoy vital expression of passion don't resort to pornographic alternatives. There simply isn't the need for it. Pornographic activity is a signal that ample passionate expression is lacking. So we gratify our desires through alternative methods.

Addiction to sports is a depiction of men's sublimation of passionate gratification. Most men lack reasonable outlets and approved methods of passionate expression, so they get their fix watching the passions of others in the sports arena. Consumerism, addiction, overwork, and depression are all manifestations of life without passion. I would venture that women proclaim "I love these shoes," more often than they say, "I love my husband." How many times have we heard the phrase "to die for" uttered in reference to some material object? What does this tell us about our sensibilities? As ridiculous as it may seem, it appears that a married person who enjoys a vigorous sex life is seen as something of an aberration in our culture.

There is a very insidious message deeply imbedded in the tapestry of our beliefs. That message is that sex is bad. It tells us that pleasure is wrong. Again I ask, "Who says so?" How can something so beautiful, so soulful be bad? Why is denial good? We must extirpate these beliefs and take a long, close look at them.

We live in a passion-less culture and more often than not, we suffer for it. Reason takes priority over passion. If however, we came to honor passion, then we could shift our definition of what we deem to be reasonable. The solution is to redirect our lives, to find and feel that which quickens our heart and makes us come alive. Passion is not scripted. It knows no boundaries, and concerns itself not with appropriateness or maturity, but with joy, spontaneity, and playfulness. It is a fervor and zest for life. It needs no analysis for it comes not from the intellect, but from the heart.

SEXUAL PASSION

Sexual passion in a committed relationship does not have to fade. If we believe that it will, that belief becomes a self-fulfilling prophecy. The inevitable decline of passion is yet another cultural myth. This is yet another circumstance of seeing what is, and concluding that is how it must be.

In the course of my work, I had occasion to talk with a man who had been married for fifteen years. When we spoke of passion and sex, he said that his sex life had almost vanished. He added, "What can you expect after all these years of marriage?" Obviously, he had accepted the myth and had written that script for himself. So how could it possibly be any different?

But what if he wrote a different script? Passion is a natural manifestation of deep intimacy. If we commit to keeping our intimacy alive, then our feelings are awake and vibrant. One result is passion. Then again, if we suppress our emotions and engender resentment by walling ourselves off, what do you suppose happens to passion? Passion does not exist in a vacuum. It is part of a healthy, intimate, and loving system of relationship. I often hear women say that when they have lost intimacy, they are no longer interested in sex. Typically, their partner complains that he isn't interested in intimacy without having their sexual needs taken care of. So we have a stalemate. No one wants to give in and both people act out an old rerun, ensuring that neither will be present to find a solution. The erroneous conclusion is that passion must die.

Uncertainty is the essence of romance.

—Oscar Wilde

As we've discussed, part of the reason for loss of passion is the boredom and predictability produced by not being present. That results from knowing it all, having the outcome all ready written. Too often sex is ordinary and passion-less. The predictability of the sexual encounter relegates it to what I call sex by appointment. Spontaneity is lost, and we fall into a routine. We can likely predict when we'll have sex since it typically takes a back seat to all of our other priorities. So if we know when and where and how we'll make love, there's little left to the imagination. We know the results in advance of the encounter. The arts of flirtation and seduction are replaced by known expectations of a sexual routine. The thrill of the unexpected gives way to a tacit agreement for a Saturday night coupling after dining out, or a movie. There is every likelihood that we return to our bedrooms and assume the same positions and relive the same experiences that define our sexual relations.

Our sexuality must open to experimentation and wonder, free from the bounds of conformity. Sex thrives with discovery and play. Here's a suggestion I recommend to recreate passion. Arrange to meet your partner at a romantic restaurant, a park, any rendez-vous will do. But it must be somewhere new, not a place either of you has been before. You must not go together. Instead travel there separately, and meet as if by chance. Now the game begins.

You're both to act as if you've never met before. This is a chance encounter. You are strangers and don't know a thing about each other. It may feel awkward at first, but stay with it. It can be very exciting. Since you've never met, you have no history together to rehash and no predictable outcomes. The box that has constrained your relationship opens. Both of you are fully present and consciously writing a new script.

Let the meeting move toward seduction. Recall the excitement of seducing and being seduced. Your complaints and resentments can be swept away in a renewed torrent of passion.

This exercise really works, but only if you play the game. If you think it's too silly or beneath you, then you're missing the spirit of it. If you can't open to this playful experience, you have opted for the absence of passion and wonder. Realize that you are writing a script of boredom and a passion-less relationship. It's your choice, what have you got to lose?

FRIENDS OR LOVERS?

Many people wonder about the importance of sexual attraction and passion. Some ask if a relationship really needs much sex anyway. Many times couples in long-standing relationships have told me that they never experienced much sexual attraction for each other. As a result there is often a profound longing in these people, a sense that there is a fundamental joy missing in their lives.

A deep sexual current between two people is an expression of their souls. Souls bare themselves to one another through the vehicle of sexual attraction. The ecstasy of sexual passion is the experience of two souls communicating in a profound and deeply resonating manner, unclothed and unmasked, radiating love.

Relationships that do not have this energy are probably not meant to be romantic love relationships. Of immense importance is the question of whether there was sufficient sexual energy in the relationship at the beginning. If it was absent from the start, these individuals were more likely meant to be friends, not lovers. If the passion was alive early on and faded with time, that might revitalize the sexual energy.

We have all heard the expression, "keeping the flames alive." Keeping the flames dancing requires tending to the fire, stoking it on occasion and adding more wood when the fire begins to subside. If we tend to our sex lives with the same care, we might very well keep the flames burning. Of course, the fuel is intimacy and the ability to be present and unscripted, without the predetermined outcomes. If we stoke the flames of passion, the fire will burn.

Passion emerges when our senses come alive. Maintaining a moribund relationship dulls them. Re-awakening wonder, playfulness, and creativity are the ingredients for a passionate life. Changing our consciousness directly influences our ability to experience and enjoy passion and sexuality.

Chapter 7

QUANTUM RELATIONSHIP

THE TRUTH

When a pickpocket looks at a saint, all he sees are pockets.
—Ram Das

As philosopher and former Harvard professor Ram Das suggests, people tend to see what they want to see. Indeed, the ancient Hebrew scripture Talmud teaches that we see things not as they are, but as we are. The point both modern and ancient sages are making is that there really is no such thing as objectivity.

No two people see the world in the same way. In other words, the truth is not out there, separate and distinct from us. We participate in creating the truth through our beliefs and feelings. There is no single, discernible truth for all to see.

We each see things in our own particular way, filtered by our own belief system and individual consciousness. If we feel love for someone, we see him or her from that perspective. If we feel disdain or anger we obviously see that person quite differently. And, as far as we're concerned, they appear as we see them.

One evening I was addressing a group of people who were going through the divorce process. One man was railing venomously against his ex-wife. From his vantage, she was a hateful, selfish human being. This was his truth. Yet, we learned that his ex had a new boyfriend, with whom she was living. Her new lover obviously didn't see her in the same hateful way. So, who is she really?

The answer is that she is infinite people, a different person as she enters into the unique energy of every different relationship. Her children, her friends, her relatives and her co-workers see her in numerous ways. Probably, she is a somewhat different person in each individual's eyes. So where is the objectivity? Is she a devoted lover or a heinous, spiteful ex-spouse? It all depends upon the particular energy of each relationship.

I recently heard a fascinating radio news report, which illuminates this concept of non-objectivity. There is a proposal for a new airport in a suburb of Houston, Texas that would place the runways right in the midst of an enormous wildlife refuge. This area is home to a wide variety of rare birds and a large population of geese.

The fight to save this refuge has brought together an alliance of two groups who would ordinarily be in dire opposition to each other: The Sierra Club and the National Rifle Association. These two organizations typically see one another in a very hostile manner. Their ideals and goals are so diametrically opposed that their perspective of each other is entirely adversarial. They naturally tend to see each other in a very fixed way. The Sierra Club is conservationist, protecting any encroachment upon nature. The NRA values individualism and the right to hunt.

Enter the proposal of a new airport and these organizations now have a common enemy. The future airport is more threatening to them than they are to each other. The NRA wants to maintain its hunting preserve and the Sierra Club wishes to save the wildlife. They actually have a common goal, the defeat of the proposed airport. Neither group changed their policies or viewpoints, yet the energy between them shifted their perspective of one another. Again we see that the objective truth is not out there, but in how we choose to see it.

We create the reality from our perspective. And every person changes based upon the different energy and dynamic of each relationship. What you feel for a person is felt by them and in turn reflected back to you. If you feel anger for them, they feel threatened and defensively reflect anger back toward you, shifting not only how you feel about them but also how you feel about yourself. Your relationship is part of a system with each person affecting the other. Thinking of each other as separate is an illusion. As soon as one's thoughts or feelings shift, the entire system of the relationship alters.

I was recently reading my son's high school report card. His science teacher commented that he was a wonderful participant and added much to the class. His math teacher wrote that he was easily distracted and disruptive. Where is the truth of my son as a student? If he had only one subject, math, we would necessarily conclude that Jesse was a mediocre student. Clearly, each teacher held a markedly different view of him. Their perspective of him is influenced by many factors. These include among other things, his enthusiasm for the subject, the time of day of the class, what my son triggers in the teacher's unconscious, how he perceives them, who sits next to him in his classroom, and an infinite list of other variables. The truth is contingent upon many things, but is, finally, quite subjective.

Love,
No matter what you feel for it,
Is still love
The object does not change the emotion
But the emotion, quite often
Changes the object
—Melba Colgrove

The visionary social scientist Gregory Bateson suggested that all things must be defined by their relationships. What Bateson meant is that nothing stands separate unto itself in a definable objectivity. We can only understand something or someone in relation to something or someone else. We are defined by our relationships. In the traditional way of seeing our partners, we perceive them as a fixed, identifiable known. We see them in a particular way. And we see ourselves as a known and concrete identity. What we hold to be true is simply the product of the energy of a particular relationship.

Consider how the chemistry you feel for another changes your perception. With the ecstasy of a love chemistry your perception of the other is full of enchantment and awe. Remove the love chemistry and the thought of the other shifts dramatically. Have they changed or has your perception changed?

The thoughts and labels that we attach to people become more than a representation. We begin to see them in a manner consistent with the label we've given them. If we know a person to be loving and nurturing, we will select those characteristics in our perception. And the tendency will be to filter out thoughts that would contradict that view. In this manner what we see tends to be self-ratifying. In other words, what we see conforms to our expectations.

It is herein that the deception lies. For we have come to know them in the way that we see them. It usually doesn't occur to us they could exist in another manner. The label that we have affixed is merely the product of the unique interactions and perceptions of the two individuals in the relationship. Moreover, that reality is subject to change the moment our perception alters.

MY TRUTH/YOUR TRUTH

We often confuse how we feel at a particular moment with being the truth. When we love someone the truth is that they are lovable. When we despise them, they are odious. The truth keeps changing. Yet we believe that truths are constant, not subject to shifting. Perhaps the problem lies in our concept of truth. If we shifted our definition of truth to state that it simply represents how we see things at this moment, then we would be much more open to see things differently in the next moment.

The truth is that when we met and fell in love, our lover was lovable. As time went on, we may have fallen out of love and our lover became unlovable. Did the truth change? Did they change? Did we change?

Everything changed, including what we call the truth. If we change our reference from *the truth* to *my truth* we would free ourselves from the defensive attachment to the absolute. It's much easier to respect another's truth when it doesn't repudiate your own.

It is the unique energy between people that determines the truth of what we see. To limit anyone with our perceptions of them is to deny that our essence is energy. We will, indeed, see them differently whenever the energy of the relationship shifts. That energy is affected by interaction with others and is always changing and evolving.

QUANTUM THINKING

No development of modern science has had a more profound
impact on human thinking than the advent of quantum theory.
—*Bryce Dewitt and Neil Graham*

Startling insights from the world of quantum physics support much of the new thinking about a nonobjective world. Even so, in our day-to-day lives most of us still see our world in terms described centuries ago by the thoughts of Sir Isaac Newton and the French philosopher René Descartes.

Descartes' position was that a purpose of science was to dominate nature. His mechanistic view decreed that a rational mind controlled the body, and that the two were separate despite causal interaction. He extended this mechanistic perspective in comparing a clock to the human body: "I consider the human body as a machine... My thought... compares a sick man and an ill made clock with my idea of a healthy man and a well made clock."

Newton told of a universe made of absolute time and absolute space. Each was independent of all else in the material world; time flowed independently of anything external.

Their ideas constructed a world that was based upon objective, observable truths. And this reality informed us that everything was separate and distinguishable from everything else. The world was machine-like, and ever more comprehensible by further reduction and analysis. Logical thinking was the deity that would enlighten us. This belief system instructed us that the observer was separate from the object being observed. The paradigm taught us that by objective observation we could know the truth of what we were studying.

In the early twentieth century, a shockingly new view of reality emerged through quantum physics. Suddenly, the infallibility of Newtonian-Cartesian reality was shaken from discoveries made in the realm of sub-atomic particles.

It was discovered, for example, that the very act of observing the particle changed its behavior. When we intrude into the sub-atomic world, the act of observation alters the object being observed. We are part of the system that we are observing. We cannot separate ourselves from that which we are observing. In fact, some contend that the particle changed its behavior to correspond with the expectations of the observer. What we look for is what we see. The notion of a detached and separate observer is hereby replaced with the concept of observer participant.

This curious phenomenon may cast some light on equally enigmatic human behaviors. If we are looking for love and good-ness in another we'll likely find those attributes. If our personal filter selects negative qualities in another person, we won't find any surprises. Our partner is, to an extent, a manifestation of our thoughts about them.

Objectivity is a myth. The very act of observing changes the observed. The observer and the observed are part of the same whole. As Margaret Wheatley, author of *A Simpler Way*, tells us, "We see the world through the self we have created." In other words, we participate in creating our reality.

Further quantum discoveries found a nonobjective, mystical reality to the interconnectedness of everything in the universe. Einstein protested this irrational and absurd notion, which even-tually induced him to utter the famous, "I can't believe that God plays dice with the universe." With this he was arguing that there was a reasoned and logical orderliness to the universe. A debate ensued for decades around a thought experiment proposed by Einstein and his colleagues. The issue was about predicting the spin of two particles, once a pair, but now separated by thousands of miles. The direction of their spins is always correlated in opposite direction of each other. In other words, if one particle has a negative spin, its twin must have a positive spin.

What would happen to the spin of particle A if the spin of its twin, particle B, was altered? According to Einstein, an instantaneous change in the spin of both particles could not occur at a great distance because nothing travels faster than the speed of light.

Danish physicist Niels Bohr, Einstein's theoretical rival, maintained that the two-particle system exists as a whole, and they are inseparable no matter how far apart. They are connected instantly. Therefore, changing the rotation of one particle would immediately be felt by the other, without any signaling necessary.

Many years later, when advances in technology finally made it possible to settle the debate once and for all, Einstein was proven wrong. John Bell, a physicist from Northern Ireland, devised a theorem which eventually demonstrated that there is an immediate connection and correlation to the spins of both particles that eludes all rational explanation. The measurement of one particle's spin immediately impacted the other's rotation, no matter how far apart they were. They were separate but part of the same whole. The universe is essentially inseparable.

INSEPARABILITY

The quantum reality is characterized by a phenomenon known as inseparability. Two particles, having interacted and then separated are now part of the same whole. Their influences upon one another create a state of inseparability, which is non-deterministic and beyond the scope of our logical minds. Once objects have interacted, they are in a sense still connected, separation being but a physical illusion.

To get a sense of this concept of interconnectedness, the "five finger exercise" of Richard Barrett, author of *Liberating Your Soul* is particularly illuminating. Richard has us imagine a place he calls "Flatland". This is a two-dimensional world with length and breadth, but no height. One morning a person living in Flatland goes out for a stroll and encounters five separate circles that have appeared mysteriously overnight. There is much consternation and excitement in Flatland, and they call in their two-dimensional scientists to analyze these amazing circles. The scientists conduct two-dimensional observations of the circles and eventually learn all there is to know about them. They record all of the data about the size and location of the circles.

Yet, there is one mystery. When force is exerted on one of the circles, the other circles begin to shift their position. This is unthinkable to the rational logic of the two-dimensional world and remains an enigma.

With a shift in consciousness they could, however, see from a three-dimensional perspective. This view would enable them to perceive that the five circles were merely imprints of the fingertips of one hand. Indeed, the circles were not separate but part of a larger whole. Such a conceptual leap in our way of perceiving reality might enable us to glimpse new potentials in our lives. If we continue to see out of the reductionist, ordered logic of the past, we will miss the greater reality. We are no more separate than the fingers of the hand.

UNCERTAINTY

Newton postulated that once we knew the location and the velocity of an object, we could predict with certainty where that object would be at a given point in the future. Quantum physics reveals that such calculations are untenable.

Uncertainty prevails and objects are quite capable of quantum leaps from one place to another, not adhering to a fixed predetermined future. Certainty has been replaced with uncertainty. The ordered logic of Newtonian thought evaporates.

This randomness presents an opportunity for limitless possibilities rather than predetermined outcomes. Our present need not be predicated upon our past. We can elect to take the quantum leap and liberate ourselves from the illusion of our past baggage. We will travel the narrow road of life from point A to point B if we believe there are no other routes available. Physics reveals that all possibilities are present and we can make quantum jumps in our lives when our consciousness avails us the opportunity.

This dramatic shift in our way of seeing can have the most profound impact upon our relationships. Our consciousness shapes our reality and is in turn influenced by the other's consciousness. Once we have interacted, we are parts of the same whole, no matter how distant in time or location.

The illusion that we are truly separate from one another is what Nick Herbert refers to as "the grand illusion" in his book, *Elemental Mind*. The illusion of separateness is based upon the belief that the entire universe is centered around one's self. There is a tendency to see reality as though everyone revolves around us, somewhat outside of our own individual consciousness.

Philosophically, this way of thinking is known as solipsism. This grand illusion might at first seem absurd. For if each of us were truly at the center of reality, there would be an infinite number of different realities. And there are. It is the denial of the other's reality that induces the myth of isolation and separation that so hinders our ability to love.

These insights from quantum physics confirm the teachings of ancient Eastern philosophers who spoke of the unity of all things and instructed that reality is a construct of the mind. We can benefit from this wisdom to awaken us to new insights about how we relate. As we begin to shift how we see and open to a reality that is participatory and interconnected, our relationships can unburden from the shackles of logical and deterministic thought that inhibit love. We think in a deterministic mode but we live in a world of randomness. It is our logic—one of our tools that we are most proud of—that may indeed deceive us. Opening to the quantum leaps of reality frees us from our mental constraints.

BELIEF SYSTEMS

All of us have a unique way of perceiving the world. Our mental models structure what we see, how we see, and how we act. We observe very selectively, based upon our belief system. Our particular belief system shapes how and what we perceive, and hence, our reality.

When our mental models become too rigid, we are locked into defensive reasoning. In our need to protect our own belief system, we react defensively when others question our assumptions. Most of the time, we deny threatening thoughts access to our awareness. Our defenses become engaged and we ward off the challenging idea. We are right and they are wrong. Our truth is superior to their truth. Unfortunately, this defensive reasoning eliminates the opportunity for learning. We insulate ourselves from seeing things differently.

Ironically, one of the most insidious myths that we inculcate is that we are open-minded. How often have you heard someone say, "I am closed-minded," or "I am not open to consider this or that"? To break through this barrier of our belief system we must first come to recognize how formidable it is and how attached we are to the reality that we have created. We come to accept as truth what are really only assumptions and representations. Yet, we must acknowledge that today's truth becomes tomorrow's folly. New insights and discoveries turn yesterday's truths into today's misconceptions. Changing insights alters our sense of reality, so we must come to acknowledge that reality is not out there somewhere in a fixed form, but a manifestation of how we choose to see.

Our belief systems are generally comprised of very pervasive value systems. They are created by the voices of our parents, leaders and socializing institutions. Although we may think that our beliefs are intrinsically our own, deeper reflection reveals otherwise. For the most part, we come to accept as truth the assumptions and values of others. And we regard these values as intrinsic truths, thereby limiting our ability to consciously choose differently. Our reality merges into the consensus opinion, and we deny our uniqueness. The belief that passion must die is such an example. This is not a truth. It is simply a commonly held belief reflecting a current value system. The belief is a product of the way that we choose to live, but certainly not an immutable truth.

In academic and professional circles we often hear the question asked, "Where were you trained?" I question why we don't ask where we were enlightened. Training suggests a continuation of the existing belief system; enlightenment encourages exploration, new learning and personal growth. Training solidifies belief systems and myths. Enlightenment, on the other hand, encourages us to greater heights of consciousness.

Let's consider the monogamy myth. Our culture instructs us that infidelity is immoral and most people accept that as the truth. Yet, what about cultures in which bigamy and polygamy are practiced? They obviously do not share the same truth. Who has the real truth? Apparently our beliefs are conditional upon many factors and it's liberating to view them in such a manner. From such perspective we can see that what we refer to as the truth is simply a product of our current belief system.

Research indicates that approximately half of all marriages encounter infidelity. In other words, a married individual is as likely to have an affair as not. Yet, when we learn of an extramarital affair, most of us react with shock or surprise. Why is that?

Logically, we might be just as surprised finding out that a marriage has not experienced infidelity. That is, after all, just as likely statistically. Yet, have you ever heard someone exclaim, "Did you hear that Jane and Bill have been faithful to each other?"

So, when infidelity causes surprise, we are reacting to the myth, which is now integrated within our belief system. There is a belief that having an affair is deviant behavior. Again this is an assumption, reflecting a value system. It is not, however, the truth. Although we may find infidelity to be morally questionable, it is illogical to conclude that it is therefore the exception to the norm. In fact, it's as much the norm as fidelity. We tend to carry with us beliefs about such behavior that evidently come from sources outside of ourselves.

When we do so we are again sleepwalking through life. This is a source of self-abandonment that contributes weightily to our struggles with mastering our lives. Our beliefs about intimacy and love are learned assumptions and patterns of thought that limit our potential for joy. The belief that soulful relationship or sustained passion in a committed relationship is merely wishful thinking engenders exactly that result. We must penetrate these beliefs to create the life that we deserve.

IT'S HARD TO CHANGE

Perhaps the greatest self-fulfilling misery comes from the belief that it's hard to change. One evening, in the midst of some exploratory dialogue in an intimacy group that I was facilitating, a woman named Susan began complaining about how difficult it was to affect positive changes in her life. In frustration she exclaimed, "Well, everyone knows how hard it is to change." I reflected a bit before responding. At the risk of not appearing supportive, I asked, "Who says so?"

Who says it's hard to change? We began to explore where this belief comes from. Everyone says it's hard to change. Yes, but who is everyone? Most people are rooted in the historical drama of their unhappiness. As we struggle to extricate ourselves, we justify being stuck with the belief it's hard to change. In other words, validating the belief justifies the misery.

Susan was stuck in her past, with a succession of failed relationships. It made sense for her to believe that it's hard to change. And as long as she believed it, it would be so. I explored this further with the group and we came to an agreement that the belief "it's hard to change" is simply an assumption. If we scrutinize the basis for this belief, all that we can conclude is that people choose to resist change. And to support their decision, they justify their unhappiness with the contention that it's hard to change.

In fact, how difficult it is to change is directly proportional to how deeply rooted that belief is. All that's required to change is that we be ready to leave our discontent behind and take responsibility for redirecting our lives. We have nothing to lose but the obstacles born of our past. As the intimacy group penetrated this myth, the question arose as to what we needed to affect change. The answer came to us as a simple three-word sentence: *I take responsibility.*

Taken a bit further, I take responsibility for directing my life. I will no longer blame people or events for my unhappiness. If my life doesn't suit me, I will change it. I will consciously write the script of my life.

The ability to reflect on our beliefs and assumptions is essential if we are to move toward the joy of intimate relationship. Our reality shifts as our insights unfold. Learning to deconstruct the way that we see frees us to attain new insights. It enables us to awaken and consciously select new behavior that will help our relationships and lives prosper.

YOU ARE WHAT YOU THINK

With these insights we can begin to shift our thoughts about how to improve our relationships. It doesn't make any sense to try to change other people. That is always a futile endeavor. The paradox prevails. The more we desire that they change, the more likely they are to resist. However, focusing on changing the energy between two people will have profound impact on the relationship. Simply altering the way we see our lover changes that person, changes us and opens the entire relationship to growth. It helps both people become unstuck. If you feel love for another you will focus on their lovable qualities. In fact, your feeling of love for them is what makes those qualities lovable. For example, a peculiar enunciation of certain words becomes music to the ear of an inspired lover. Remove the loving aura and the same sounds might now resemble chalk grating on the blackboard.

Our own thoughts mislead us when they report in to us about the objective truth out there. Thought takes the position that it's merely observing what is. This is entirely deceptive. Our thought participates in creating our reality. If we consider the impact that our thoughts have on our state of relationship, we can see that our partner becomes who we see them to be.

It is our perception that creates the reality. In a relationship that is angry and conflicted, the filter of antagonism will create continued negativity. Trying to get your partner to change will likely meet with more resistance and defensive behavior, which in turn will be seen as more negativity. And so you both spiral downward. But all of that loveless energy shifts the moment that one of you decides to see differently.

THE QUANTUM LAKE

I was taking a bike ride one morning when I came across a small lake I had passed many times in my car. The slower pace of the bike induced me to stop and reflect a while on this beautiful autumn morning. I sat on a bench near the water, a lush tree hanging just overhead. The sun was bright, reflecting on much of the lake. It had rained heavily the night before and a strong breeze was moving through. As it did, drops of water fell from the tree, penetrating the part of the lake closest to me. As I focused on that area, it all seemed rather incongruous. The sun was so brilliant yet raindrops appeared to be falling. I shifted my gaze toward the middle of the lake where no precipitation fell, but the water was undulating from the effect of the wind. Wherever I chose to look, I created a different reality in this lake. Yet, these were both parts of the same whole.

I began to consider that there were two entirely different events occurring simultaneously in this lake. As I thought about this, I looked at the most distant part of the lake. There I saw neither rippling water nor raindrops. Only stillness. At the very least, I perceived three markedly different events in this lake. Wherever I looked I was likely to see a different aspect of the lake.

It occurred to me that the reality or the truth would be found wherever I happened to focus. One lake, yet so many different nuances. And so it is with our sense of self and our perception of others. We are like the Quantum Lake. An infinite number of feelings, thoughts, and attitudes. The complex that we select at any particular moment becomes our truth. If we focus upon a particular thought, with its incumbent emotions, that thought will shape how we see ourselves and our partners. At any given time, we can select any particular viewpoint of another person, but we must acknowledge that we have missed the places where we didn't look. The expression, "There's more than meets the eye," is an adroit insight. We tend to see what we choose to see.

WHAT WE LOOK FOR IS WHAT WE SEE

David Bohm, the renowned physicist said that a new way of seeing is more important than an increase in knowledge. We don't need more information; we need to see differently. One of the most powerful things in the universe comes from the enlightenment of insight.

Some of your partner's traits that now repel you are probably the same characteristics that once attracted you. They haven't changed. But the energy between you has, and the perspective creates the reality. If one of you lets go of the objective truth that you are so vehemently attached to, it may free you to select something different to see.

The exercise that I suggest is to think back to when you first fell in love with your partner. Recall a trait of theirs that you appreciated. Now, find that characteristic again. It's still there somewhere. Get in touch with how it used to make you feel and permit yourself to experience it. Share the feeling with your partner. This is not an intellectual endeavor, and it has nothing to do with right and wrong, or changing one's behavior. It's really much deeper. When we are in touch with feelings of love, the other issues lose importance. Remember that the truth is not out there somewhere. It is in your own consciousness. That is what creates your world and your reality.

*The same consciousness that created a
problem can never solve that problem.*
—*Albert Einstein*

When we come to understand the power of our thoughts we can open to the infinite possibilities of relationship. We are, literally, what we think. Just consider the immense power that our thoughts have in creating the reality of our dream state. They script an entire drama and summon into creation all of the actors and events for us. With the exception of the lucid dreamer, we are immersed in the absolute reality of the dream, everything emanating from our thoughts. Our waking experience is not entirely dissimilar. Typically we are at one with our thoughts and don't take the opportunity to witness them. The thoughts that we select create our truth and our emotional state.

The greatest leverage for change comes from detaching from our thoughts. By learning to observe our thoughts, we can separate from them and choose different realities. When we do so, we are no longer one with the thought, so we may question what the thought is telling us. Our thoughts try to tell us that they know it all. But as we have seen, this can be deceiving. It is helpful if we come to see our thoughts merely as our own representations of what is, as opposed to the reality itself.

As we learn to step out of the scripted reruns of our relationship, we can choose new ways that no longer determine the outcome in advance, but permit ourselves and our partners to select more consciously. These changes in perception open the box that the relationship has been confined to. We put up the walls in the first place; we can take them down in a moment.

This lesson once again reveals the paradox. We can affect immediate change in another person by changing our thoughts. Any change in one person must affect a change in the other person. For they are now in a relationship with a somewhat different person. And the good news is that the moment we change the energy, our relationship is altered. A subtle shift in your perception can have a dramatic effect on the relationship and of course, your partner's perception of you will change. So the issue of how to get things unstuck is addressed by looking into ourselves and shifting our thoughts.

With a small change in thought we might witness a significant shift in the relationship. You know the feeling you have when there are dozens of thoughts racing through your mind, each clamoring for attention?   You choose which thought to attach to, and within moments the emotions are summoned from your memory bank that fit that thought. This is an unconscious process. The feelings that attach to the thought are part of the conditioned reflex pattern of our behavior. And they are almost without exception a product of past memories and feelings. The thought and the feeling are part of the same system; they are inseparable. Once summoned into consciousness, the feeling will then evoke more thought consistent with that feeling. This is why we find ourselves in emotional cycles that spiral up or down.

The difference between a happy life and an unhappy
life is a matter of the thoughts we choose.

A former client, Dan, related this story: He and his ex-wife live in adjacent towns and Dan often spots her car on local roads. The instant Dan recognized her exact model and color car he glanced down at the license plate to see if it was in fact her. Although it wasn't, he had conjured a mental image of her license number. A moment later, Dan's memory bank of emotions scripted a feeling from deep in his past.

In fact, it had little to do with his ex-wife. It turned out that his reaction was directly related to a conversation that she once had with him about another person with whom he had ended a love affair. Simply imagining her license plate created an emotional state that drew him back to some past sorrow. His reaction had nothing at all to do with his ex-wife. Dan's thoughts had produced a tumultuous reaction. He found himself once again mourning the loss of a lover simply because of a thought about a license plate that connected him to the memory of that lover. The thoughts that he selected scripted a painful emotional state for him. Although his anxiety was produced from an erroneous thought about a license plate, his discord felt very real.

Another client, Stan, shared with me his recurring worries about money. He constantly obsessed about his financial woes. He fretted about how he'd pay the bills and meet his future obligations. As we delved into the connection between thought and feeling, Stan came to realize that almost immediately after selecting the thought about money, he had induced a state of anxiety. Stan had created this distress. In this emotional state he was powerless to focus on solutions. In fact, his increased anxiety only spiraled him further into fearful thoughts.

He was, however, free to choose differently. I asked Stan how it would feel if he chose thoughts about improving his circumstances rather than on thoughts that obsessed solely on the problem. We explored different remedies to his financial hardships, some of which seemed entirely plausible to Stan. I asked him how he felt when he consciously selected these thoughts. He said he had an entirely different experience. His veil of doom faded and he had glimpses of optimism. Stan focused on the solutions rather than the problem.

Moreover, he had created a new emotional reality that would better incline him to produce these changes in his life. Nothing outside of him had changed other than the thoughts he selected.

THE THOUGHTS WE SELECT CREATE THE SELF THAT WE ARE

I am not suggesting that we avoid or deny unpleasant realities; however, the ability to detach from the thought frees us emotionally so that we may witness the mind-set that is creating the unpleasant edge to our reality. Once we detach from the emotional discomfort, we are better able to consciously deal with the problem at hand.

In his visionary book, *Thought as a System*, David Bohm teaches that our thoughts are fragmentary; they trick us into thinking that we are separate from others. Thoughts break things down in a piecemeal fashion and disconnect us from the bigger picture. Our mind tends to look at symptoms rather than the interconnecting system. Only by looking at the flow of the larger system can we begin to see from where the problems emerge.

Bohm continues by explaining that the paradox is that the symptoms are generated by the very thought that we must observe in a detached manner. In our relationships we tend to draw conclusions about others rather than step outside the thought and witness it. The all-knowing tendency of our thoughts creates a massive misconception. We confuse our thought with the truth, about our partners and ourselves.

If your partner does something that pushes your button and you select the immediate accompanying thought, the emotions that attach with that thought are recalled from past experiences. Therefore, the past is really summoned into the present. Bohm adds "Thought creates a problem and then tries to do something about it while continuing to make the problem, because it doesn't know what it is doing. It's a bunch of reflexes working."

And once again you are no longer in the present, attentive and aware. You are somewhere in the memory banks, creating a future similar to the past. You are, however, free to step back and witness your selection of thought. As you begin to do so, you can reflect upon the manner in which you create your drama.

THE DRAMA

Each of us scripts the drama that we call our life. The tendency is to believe that the things, events and people in our lives are impacting on us and we are simply reacting to them. We may complain that we're unhappy because of our lovers, parents, work or friends. We believe that all of these forces lie somewhere outside of us, separate and distinct from us. We often feel powerless as we struggle to control these external factors.

Typically, we have summoned them into our drama and then blame them for our unhappiness. If we make another person responsible for our happiness, we are subverting ourselves and dooming the relationship. This becomes especially clear when we look for the other to change. We think that if only they would change one thing or another, then we would be happy. We are writing the script for unhappiness the moment that we think that way.

This drama will surely keep us from happiness, for it's unreasonable to expect someone else to change. It would better serve us to ask ourselves why we couldn't accept them for exactly who they are. If we chose a partner who didn't fully suit us, what does that tell us about the drama we wrote? We might ask ourselves how our selection of partners informs us about our own sense of what we deserve. We were opting for discontent from the start, but we don't see it that way and we continue to fault the other person for our frustration. The dramas that we live obscure our truth and keep us externalized. They are symptomatic of sleepwalking through life, inattentive and unaware.

This sleepwalking involves us in the drama, but doesn't inform us that we are writing the script. It's very easy to get caught up in our dramas. In fact, I recall an episode that occurred toward the end of a relationship that I was in. I was waiting at a park for her to arrive for a picnic. Although we loved each other very much there were several stressful issues in our relationship that didn't permit the opportunity for the joy that I deserved. I had been setting myself up for prolonged pain and had become accustomed to it.

She was very late for our appointment and I found myself pacing up and down the driveway, looking over my shoulder at each approaching car. As time went by, I became more agitated. Then, in one particular instant, when I turned to look at the next car and realized it again wasn't her, it dawned on me that I was pleased. Her lateness would justify my continued anger. I had detected a deeper component within myself that had acclimated to my painful drama. I asked myself why I had chosen to participate in a relationship that brought me such anguish. In that instant, I stopped blaming her and I stepped out of my drama.

OUR INNER DIALOGUE PAINTS
THE OUTER CANVAS

We must remove ourselves from the event, from the drama, so that we can consciously make our choices. Ask yourself what the major themes of your life are. What keeps you from happiness? The answer reveals the drama. Underscoring most life dramas is a fundamental sense of what we feel we deserve. Once we identify our drama, we must ask ourselves what our personal belief systems are that produced that particular drama. Our beliefs about others and ourselves are the ingredients for our life's struggles. If we focus solely on the struggle, we are simply looking at the symptom. In all likelihood, that drama may be replaced by another one. Living life without awakening induces us to deal with the crises and events without even noticing that we're orchestrating them ourselves. In order to transform our lives and create happiness, we must penetrate the personal belief system that created the drama.

Dana was an attractive young woman in her mid-thirties suffering from a succession of failed relationships. She had experienced a divorce and two conflicted relationships within a year's time. Her drama was replete with issues about the shortcomings of her partners. I asked Dana what she wanted in her life, and she replied that she was in quest of a fulfilling relationship. That was her vision, but her drama was about men who disappointed her and the ensuing conflict. I explored Dana's personal belief systems with her and we uncovered her core belief. She confessed, "I'm not good enough." This self-critique had been with her since childhood. Dana felt that she didn't deserve happiness. It was not surprising that she had selected inappropriate partners so that her drama would fulfill her belief system about herself.

This self-fulfilling prophecy was, of course, unconscious. By making her core beliefs about herself more conscious, Dana could step back and observe her behavior. She would then be able to step out of her drama and take responsibility for her life.

If we are living in pain or deprivation, we likely have inner issues about what we really deserve. We must stop blaming forces outside of ourselves and release the drama. Fortunately, the life that we are living provides us with many clues that can help us discover how we are unconsciously writing the script of our life.

Much of this life drama emanates from our personal belief system. We can, however, liberate ourselves at any moment to recreate our lives. Remember that we make up life as we go along. Stepping out of the drama frees us to see things differently and choose a different script. The more that we can observe our thoughts and come into a state of conscious being with ourselves, the easier it is to remove ourselves from our drama. Although people and circumstances may cause us pain or disappointment, the real pain comes not from the event, but from how we choose to see it. I could have continued to victimize myself as the hapless lover or I could have written a new script. Dana could continue to suffer at the hands of her inadequate partners or she could free herself from her self-imposed bondage of pain.

Jane and her husband Mark came to see me after eight years of an unfulfilling marriage. Mark had been a very controlling partner and Jane had obediently acquiesced. They had decided to separate and were looking for my confirmation that this path seemed sensible. Since they had no recollection of ever being in love, it appeared that their decision to separate was, in fact, reasonable. And so they did.

Six months after they separated Jane came in to see me. Although she was thriving during this period and enjoying greater happiness than ever before, she was concerned that she was making a mistake. During this time Jane had vowed to herself that she would never again be dominated by a partner. She proclaimed that she deserved to be in love. Yet, she hesitated about her decision. Maybe her marriage wasn't so bad after all, she thought. In fact, she said she was considering reconciling with Mark.

I asked Jane if she felt that she could ever be in love with Mark. Jane responded with a convincing no. I pointed out that the conflict between what she claimed she wanted in her life—love—and her behavior were entirely at odds. Jane's declarations about what she said she deserved in her life and her thoughts about reconciliation created a powerful dissonance in her. When we say one thing and do another we must look at beliefs that keep us from our happiness. Jane's drama was a manifestation of her belief that she didn't deserve to be in love.

THE BIG PICTURE

Countless reports of near death experiences recount people who indicate having seen their entire life pass before them. Some say that it was similar to watching a very fast newsreel of their lives. Such a visualization is helpful in removing ourselves from the drama.

When we are so steeped in the energy and conflict of our dramas we lose the ability to perceive the bigger picture. The stories that we tell ourselves become our excuse for not living life with purposeful intent. These stories keep us from seeing clearly. I suggest that we imagine our next moment as the last instant of our lives. If we then viewed our lives in retrospect, at a distance from the drama, we might ask ourselves if our life made sense. Were we living self-actualized lives in a purposeful way and committed to happiness? Or were we lost in the events of the powerless drama?

At times our fantasies keep us embroiled in our dramas. Fred was married to a very angry woman, named Claire, who was incapable of showing any affection or love. Claire tended to be verbally and emotionally abusive toward Fred while he clung to the hope that Claire would change. Fred continued to fantasize that Claire would see the light and love him in an appropriate manner. Fred seized upon any kind overture by Claire as justification for staying in the marriage. The reality of their marriage was that Claire made no commitment to improve their relationship and Fred had no realistic expectation that things might get better. Still, he clung to his fantasy.

His fantasy provided him with an escape. Fantasies produce endorphins, a biochemical simulation of euphoria similar to how one feels after vigorous exercise. As Fred fantasized Claire to be a loving wife, he was warmed with the comfort of that thought. It served as a security blanket, enveloping him and distancing him from the anxiety of the truth.

Fred's drama was that he was not loved or appreciated by his wife and was always feeling inadequate. Fred suggested that he was having difficulty leaving Claire because he was addicted to her. I told Fred that he wasn't really addicted to Claire but to his fantasy. It was anesthetizing him from the pain of his drama. Fred's underlying belief system was that he didn't deserve to be loved. In this instance, his fantasy served to keep him in his drama.

I had Fred imagine himself as a prisoner confined to a cell. Claire was the prison guard, responsible for his containment. Fred spent many years in this cell, all the while hoping that Claire would come to recognize him as faultless and thereby release him. Of course, this never happened. One day, Fred finds Claire asleep outside his cell and the cell gate has been left open. Fred's opportunity for escape is at hand, yet he decides that he'll wait for Claire to awaken so that he can prove to her that he's really blameless. So Fred stays in his cell and continues to blame Claire for his unhappiness.

The drama becomes the justification for why we aren't happy. Although we may say that we deserve to be happy, our actions indicate otherwise. If we step back from the conflict, we see how the dramas of two people interface. In the case of Fred and Claire, we have two people who are committed to being unhappy. Claire is invested in her anger. She has difficulty maintaining healthy relationships and projects her inner turmoil onto others, venting at them. Fred's belief system instructs him that he doesn't really deserve to have a loving intimate relationship. These people have dramas perfectly suited for one another. In fact, unless someone changes, they are simply manifesting their belief systems through their relationship with one other.

Fred unconsciously chooses to be punished and imprisoned, so it would make sense that he would select an abusive partner. Claire requires a submissive passive partner so that she might have a partner upon whom to vent her rage. Lost in the particulars of their conflict is the bigger picture. Their dramas have summoned one another into their respective lives.

I often ask my clients, "What does it feel like to be you? If I could hear your inner dialogue, what would it sound like?" I'm referring to that most intimate and private conversation that you have with yourself. It is here that you create the self that you are. The people and events in your life are but manifestations of this inner dialogue.

Listen to your inner dialogue and you will begin to perceive how your thoughts create your reality. The difference between a happy life and an unhappy life is simply the thoughts we choose. The ability to observe our thoughts and behavior assists us in awakening our consciousness and redirecting our lives.

QUANTUM RELATIONSHIP

As we begin to shift our perspective and release our thoughts about reality and the truth, we enter into the realm of quantum thinking. Quantum Thinking opens the doorway to Quantum Relationship. This quantum way of seeing is the antithesis of deterministic thinking. Event A does not cause event B; rather, they have an effect on one another. Each is part of the same whole. Just as two protons come together and are forever changed by their interaction, no matter how distant, we are part of a new energy once we have related to another person.

As with the Quantum Lake, what we see is predicated upon where we look, and what we are looking for. Quantum Relationship redirects our attention to our energy, for it is there that happiness may be found. Our partner is, in part, who they are because of the manner in which we see them and what our perception confers on them.

A fundamental cause of our discontent is the confusion that abounds in our reverence for logical thought. We have made logic our deity and cling to it in the face of non-logical quantum phenomena. The quantum reality appears strange because of our reverence for rational thought. The paradox lies not in the reality but in our conception of what reality should be. Logical determinism is destructive to soulful energy and thwarts matters of the heart. Predictive outcomes and deterministic behavior are not only soul defeating, they are conspirators in creating loveless relationships. Such thinking removes the playfulness and spontaneity from life.

When we live our lives as though things are fixed, we block the natural wonder of the harmonious dance of all things. Quantum randomness opens us to the limitless opportunity of willful choice, free of predetermined outcomes. It enables us to script wonder and enchantment into each moment, irrespective of past experiences. We can create new realities in each instant. Quantum Relationship honors the magic of love.

Chapter 8

RE-CREATING YOUR LIFE

To venture causes anxiety, but not to venture is to lose one's self.
And to venture in the highest is precisely to be conscious of one's self.
—Soren Kierkegaard

Our ascension to higher levels of consciousness enlightens us, propelling us to recreate our lives in a purposeful manner so that joy may be ours. Although we are constantly creating our lives, the quantum leap of inner-directed consciousness permits us new levels of awareness so that we may script our lives and relationships in our highest purpose. The transition from the vision-less drama in which we are reacting to events and people, to the mastery of joyful relationship requires a commitment to learning. The elements of this process are embodied in self-mastery. Mastery empowers us to come into conscious relationship with our lovers and ourselves.

MASTERY

Self-mastery is the ability to consciously make choices in a manner consistent with our soul's purpose. It is masterful to focus, with intent, upon a meaningful life, one in which we may create our vision and release our obstacles as we move toward it. Mastery is developing the insight and the skills to embrace that which enhances our lives and to reject that which diminishes us. The clarity of understanding the difference between enhancement and diminishment, and acting purposefully in that regard, is the key to joyful life.

At certain times in life we must ask ourselves, "Does this enhance or diminish my life?" Ordinarily, the answer is perfectly clear. Our heart knows at once. If we choose that which diminishes us we have written the script for unhappiness. We may offer a multitude of excuses as to why we are permitting someone or something to detract from us, but by doing so we are remaining enmeshed in the drama. We are blinded by the story we're telling ourselves. We are not the masters of our lives when we offer excuses for our lack of joy. Living with anything that diminishes us is a product of fear. The underlying belief system is that we don't deserve better. This is a reactive life devoid of empowering vision.

Developing the acuity to clarify the difference between enhancement and diminishment releases us from the drama and emboldens us to make the vision come alive. Once we have taken the steps toward our own responsibility, free from the inclination to project our inner disquiet onto our partner, we are finally in a position to determine whether or not the relationship replenishes or drains us. When we choose that which enhances us we are creating life from love.

I TAKE RESPONSIBILITY

Mastery is a process of commitment to insight. It permits us to master the lower self so that the higher self can consciously write a script for love and intimacy. It is a repudiation of need and blame and an affirmation of responsibility and insight. Self-mastery is the realization of our innate power. This is not a power based upon fear or manipulation of others. It has nothing to do with control or domination. It is a power that cannot be taken from us. It is the power to recreate our lives. As the sculptor constantly reshapes an emerging piece of art, we must do the same with our lives. Mastery is the process of developing the skills to live well, with purpose and commitment. Herein lies the vessel for loving intimacy and joy.

The mantra of self-mastery is I take responsibility. My life is not about blaming people or things for my unhappiness. I am the creator of my destiny. I embrace the adventure of my life. Mastery crafts a masterpiece out of life.

VISION STATEMENT

An essential component of mastery is vision. A start-up business creates a business plan in order to focus its agenda for success. It serves as a guide for the goals of the business. The plan elucidates what must be accomplished for those goals to be realized.

We need such a plan for our lives. Rather than meander through life chasing after an elusive joy, we must be present and focus on what happiness looks like.

The practice of visioning can help you see that plan. The act of creating our manifesto for a happy and joyful life is a pledge to ourselves that we will not permit life to just happen. The vision statement is a living document which must regularly undergo reflection and change as we experience and grow. The vision statement should reflect the needs of our soul, not the fears of our personality. In the moment when life is over and we depart from our bodies, the question will be , "Did I live my life well, without regrets?" The purpose of our statement of vision is to provide an affirmative response to that question.

Shortly after I graduated college I had a precognition of what life might offer if I wasn't diligent in my course of consciousness. I likened life to the luggage conveyor at the airport. Once on the conveyor, the suitcase just goes on the ride, round and round, without choice as to its destination. And so it seemed with life, one decision implying the next course of action, with increasingly less opportunity to create the life that I wanted. I promised myself that every so often I would jump off the conveyor of life and ask, "Is this what I had in mind, does this suit me, or do I need to make some changes?" I didn't have a vision statement yet, but I surely had a concern about my ability to consciously create my life.

The vision statement must be more than a reflection of the goals of one's life as a means to an end. It is intended more to reflect the basic purpose of our lives. Peter Senge, author of the groundbreaking *The Fifth Discipline*, shares his insights about vision and mastery. "The ability to focus on ultimate intrinsic desires, not only on secondary goals, is a cornerstone of personal mastery." Although Senge's work is devoted to learning organizations, his insights are most valuable in any discussion of personal happiness and contribute powerfully to self-mastery.

The vision leads us to our greater destiny: intimacy and love. As we have seen, achievements and accomplishments devoid of deeper meaning leave us unfulfilled. The vision helps to clarify how we need to live to be in harmony with our souls. This is a statement of our love, work, interests and our passion. It is our reason for being.

A vision statement identifies the life we were meant to live and then clears the path for that undertaking. In so doing, it fully engages the soul. If we know what our deeper callings are, then the statement demonstrates whether we are on the proper road to our joy. Moreover, if we are not clear about our purpose—as many of us aren't—it then serves to focus us inward toward our greater truths.

SHARED VISION

The vision, therefore, is our plan for life. But it is a plan that requires regular re-visitation. Include in your statement all things and ideals important to you. They may be as simple as enjoying nature, engaging in physical activities or pursuing your hobbies. Or they may be as complex as finding your soul mate, or helping humankind. Once you have written your statement, inscribe it within a circle. If you are in a relationship with another person or considering a commitment to another, shared vision is a wonderful technique for determining potential compatibility. Shared vision is yet another concept put forth by Peter Senge, in his work with learning organizations. If each of your statements is enclosed in a circle, the area of overlap is what I refer to as shared vision. This is a particularly powerful exercise for people contemplating marriage.

If we find adequate overlap in vision, we might assume that we have at least enough of a shared vision of happiness to pursue a relationship. However, if there is a decided lack of overlap, we might question why this couple is in a relationship. Lack of shared vision usually results in arguments around selfishness. For example, David enjoys rigorous exercise, mountain climbing and a very active social life. His girlfriend Anne is rather sedentary. She finds her delight in cooking dinners for two and reading poetry by the fireplace. Although they may be in love at the moment, their lives will likely unfold in conflict around who is being selfish about what they want to do. Neither is being selfish. They simply enjoy different things. The bigger question is, should they be planning on spending a life together?

We often come into conflict with our lovers because of a discrepancy in regard to expectations. Our visions reveal what we expect out of life. With a reasonable amount of shared vision, there is an agreed upon plan for fulfillment. It is very important to review your statement of vision periodically to ensure that your lives are being lived in accordance with your vision. For example, if a couple agree that quiet reflective time at home is in their vision, and they find themselves on the fast track at work, they must ask at what cost? They have likely lost their path. This might occasion a dialogue about the purpose of their lives and catalyze a shift in their decision making process. In effect, they need to jump off the conveyor belt and take charge of their lives. They are the masters, not the servants.

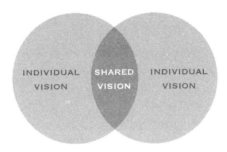

Ultimately, the most important component of shared vision may simply be a matter of congruence of consciousness. If our level of consciousness resonates, if we see things in a manner that harmonizes with each other, the smaller details may be worked out. The question is do we tune out or tune in to one another? You may both like to ski and bike ride, but if you have dissimilar expectations about what reasonable levels of honesty and intimacy are, the outcome is rather predictable. Two people who are in accord that intimacy is vital to their happiness and have agreed upon the definition of the word, have the deepest of shared vision. From this basis the exploration into the particulars proceeds in a natural course.

Anniversaries should be the greatest ceremony of intimacy, a celebration of a life shared in commitment to our deepest fulfillment. A review of our vision statement gives us the opportunity to reflect and share with one another the most poignant and intimate details of our hopes and dreams and assists us in creating our lives consciously.

CREATIVE TENSION

Peter Senge continues his visionary work by delineating the difficulties people encounter when their visions are some distance from their current reality. Although there may be a sense of one's vision, the current reality may evoke mediocrity or a sense of hopelessness due to a large gap between the two. Senge refers to this gap as creative tension. He has us imagine a rubber band stretched between current reality and vision. When the rubber band is stretched, the result is tension. He suggests that there are only two alternatives here: resolution or release.

We can move our reality toward the vision—utilizing creative tension in this direction—or we can release the vision and accept the current reality. If our visions have evaporated and we are succumbing to either the mediocrity or despair of our current reality, we have likely opted for much less than we deserve. This choice typically results in depression. The prevalence of anti-depressants in our culture is testament to our loss of vision.

The ability to perceive our current reality, in relation to our vision, is essential in self-mastery. Utilizing the creative tension to move us inexorably toward our vision is a manifestation of our awakening consciousness. We are then using the tension creatively as we redirect our lives toward the vision. Stepping out of the drama and taking responsibility for our being propels us toward our vision.

We may think of our current reality as reflecting the state of our personality, but as we've seen, the personality typically disguises the loving nature of the soul. Born of neediness and deficits, the personality is reactive and powerless, masked and wanting. In this condition, vision is hard to come by. In a state of fear we resist change. We are too busy just trying to deal with life. We are reacting rather than creating.

Vision is the voice of the soul. When we envision our purpose we are accessing our deeper truths and instructing our personality as to the life we were destined to live. In this consciousness we see change as a tool for our self-empowerment. Vision permits our personality to reflect our soul, radiating in love and intimacy. The most profound intimacy occurs when we are in harmony with our deepest self.

THE BUTTERFLY

Recreating our lives with integrity may require that we experience discomfort. The avoidance of such painful struggle limits our opportunity for growth. Yet that very tendency to evade uncomfortable situations leaves us in far worse condition. It renders us incapable of mastering our lives. If our energy is directed at fending off change and running from struggle, then we have opted to be imprisoned by our circumstances.

The following story recently forwarded to me beautifully describes the dynamic between struggle and growth.

A man found the cocoon of a butterfly. One day a small opening appeared; he sat and watched the butterfly for several hours as it struggled to force its body through that little hole. Then it seemed to stop making any progress. It appeared as if it had gotten as far as it could. It could go no further.

So the man decided to help the butterfly. He took a pair of scissors and snipped off the remaining bit of the cocoon. The butterfly then emerged easily. But it had a swollen body and small, shriveled wings.

The man continued to watch for a while because he expected that at any moment the wings would enlarge and expand to be able to support the body.

It never happened. In fact, the butterfly spent the rest of its life crawling around with a swollen body and shriveled wings. It was never able to fly.

What the man, in his kindness and haste, did not understand was that the restricting cocoon and the butterfly's struggle to free itself were God's way of forcing fluid from the body of the butterfly into its wings so that it would be ready for flight.

Sometimes struggles are exactly what we need in our life. If God allowed us to go through life without any obstacles, it would cripple us. We would not be as strong as we might have been. And we could never fly.

Chapter 9

SOULFUL RELATIONSHIP

& SOULFUL SEX

DISCOVERY

When we take the sum of our very limited life experiences and equate that with the total potential of life, we have limited ourselves to a future that replicates our past. An existence based upon fear of change inclines us to have the answers in advance and then induces us to live our lives in that self-fulfilling prophecy. We conform to the rules that tell us how to relate and how to live and we abandon wonder and enchantment for the sake of correctness and productivity. This belief system discourages experimentation and playfulness. It directs us through life with blinders on, causing us to miss the joy that lies just beyond our vista. This paradigm is so severely limiting that it makes our souls cry. It paralyzes us through regimentation and conformity. This is relationship without intimacy, life without love. Such life is without authenticity and integrity.

Life emerges by opening to discovery. Embracing exploration enables us to continuously learn and create. Again we might look at our lives as a sculptor approaches his craft. The self that we know and the relationships that we have are constantly being reshaped. New crafting creates new opportunities. If the old model suited us for a time but our growth and needs have shifted, we must re-craft the sculpture. And so it is with our lives. If we view them as ever-changing and open to new discovery, they awaken and thrive.

Relationship without discovery is paralysis. If we have cut ourselves off from any new learning, we have gone to sleep. When we presume that the answers to our relationships already exist, we stop experimenting and looking for new ways. We focus on solutions and outcomes and entirely miss the process. We are looking at the destination and are depriving ourselves of the journey of life. That journey contains the riches of discovery, celebration and wonder. They are the ingredients of soulful relationship.

WONDER

We must open to wonder and enchantment and immerse ourselves in play if we are to thrive. It is the loss of wonder and enchantment that leads to the loss of passion. We have looked at the wonder that was present when we first met, how alive we felt, present in the moment. But all too soon, we knew it all, because the way that we came to relate to another left us closed to new learning. There was nothing left to discover. We closed the door to enchantment and created relationships that were dull and boring. The way that we live our lives and structure our relationships makes wonder absent. And it makes our lives gray and passion-less.

Let's consider the word wonderful. Wonderful, as originally intended, refers to something or someone full of wonder. It is a feeling of extraordinary awe or marvel. It's what love first felt like, an experience or feeling that words could not describe. It was an energy from the heart and the soul that took us to someplace magical.

But consider the current use of the word wonderful: "you did a wonderful job on that report," or "that's wonderful," as a response to a piece of good news. Are we saying that the promotion, or the report or the good grades are things full of marvel? Obviously not. We are applying a stamp of excellence, a job well done. Wonderful has come to mean competent.

Wonder is no longer honored in our culture. We respect performance and achievement, surpassing goals and replacing them with new ones. And this turning away from wonder is a fundamental reason for loss of love and passion. This is an act of infidelity to our souls.

We live in a culture so devoid of reverence for such matters that we suffer as a result. Relationships have become business like partnerships in which we have roles and obligations to fulfill. These relationships more closely resemble an efficient management team than a loving experience in sacred union. Countless times I have worked with couples who have said that they have good working partnerships. They say that they work well together.

But, they don't love well together. They are discontented because efficiency is not enough. Their souls are not being nourished. There is no wonder in these relationships. The priority in most relationships is about getting the job done. We devote ourselves to building careers and living a productive life. But at what cost? The gems of life are missed because we are looking in the wrong places.

Wonder was the domain of childhood, an integral part of imagination and awe. The child could play with wonder as an exploration of fantasy and utilize it as grounding for growth and well-being. Time stood still. A life full of wonder is a life of reverence. Our universe is full of wonder. Life itself is wonder. But all too soon we teach our children that they are acting like children. They must grow up, and give up wonder. And similarly, as adults we have abandoned ourselves as we cut ourselves off from awe and wonder. We cannot honor our lovers and ourselves in the absence of wonder. Love is a wonder. And wonder takes the mundane and makes it sacred.

The presence of wonder makes us one with the other. If a breathtaking sunset or the marvel of a lover's touch creates wonder, we are no longer separate. Our boundaries melt away and we open to the marvelous connection to another soul. When we are separate from the other, we take that person for granted. Our partner begins to exist outside of our sphere and our love. We are living again under the grand illusion of separateness. Wonder is creative, expansive and loving. The absence of wonder is constricting and soul-less.

For relationship to thrive, for passion to be present, wonder and enchantment must be honored. We must be more childlike and take ourselves less seriously. To re-awaken wonder we have to become more playful and commit to cherish and worship our heart and soul, the only authentic source of happiness. Love is playful.

CELEBRATION

Life is an opportunity to celebrate. Yet we wait for our calendars to indicate when we may celebrate. We are indoctrinated to believe that there are appropriate times to celebrate, as if we need the excuse of New Year's Eve to make us merry. Living with a consciousness that instructs us that Valentine's Day is the appropriate time to honor romance and love is absolutely absurd. Our souls don't require permission to celebrate. If we extirpate ourselves from the numbness of our regimented lives, we can awaken to the fact that there is much to celebrate at any moment. And the more we shift into a reverence for life, the more we discover to revere. It is everywhere we look. When we get out of our own way, life unfolds.

SOULFUL RELATIONSHIP

Wonder and awe create the opportunity for soulful relationship. Soulful relationship can and will emerge when we have grown into conscious relationship. When the needs of our fear-based, masked personality recede before the emergence of our souls, partnership between loving souls can flourish. Such relationship can only occur when we welcome change and honor personal growth and commitment. We cannot enjoy soulful relationship with another until we encourage our own soul to radiate.

The journey from the masked personality into the riches of the soul is essential in creating conscious relationship. It is only from our wholeness that we may resonate with another. When our personality mirrors our soul, we may unconditionally and fully revere another. This transition into sacred union has no place for fear. Love reigns supreme in this palace. Picture a tuning fork just struck. Imagine both ends of the instrument vibrating in perfect unity, their energies in harmony, reflecting and accentuating the other. This is soulful relationship. Such relationship honors spirit and growth. It treats the other as sacred which in turn permits us to bask in the reverence of soulful relationship. In order to reach this state of soul partnership, we must first take our own inner paths toward personal mastery and commitment to learning and change.

We are energy. Love is fearless energy. All else is illusion. For two souls to communicate in loving harmony, we must permit our energy to come forth in all of its power. It is this energy that we refer to as soulful, for the soul is energy. When we say that love is a feeling, an electrical feeling, we are speaking of a love energy. Fear blocks any such opportunity for conscious relationship. Our energies are obstructed by the callous boundaries of masks and social conventions.

If we are to commit to soulful relationship, we must enter into our most vulnerable being. For it is here that the soul lives. Our hearts will lead us into this realm of soulful love. Soulful partnership is an organic process, free of the toxins that devour our highest purpose. When we have liberated ourselves from our old way of seeing, we can emerge consciously and bask in the glory of the soul. Two souls fully engaged vibrate in an ethereal manner that disintegrates boundaries. Their energies, once separate, now form a new entity. A being is created out of this transformation. Whereas before there was only you and me, now there is us. Once these energies have interacted, nothing will ever be the same. Here we witness the quantum inseparability.

Yet, there can be no ownership in soulful relationship. Consciousness does not honor fear-based behavior and the constraints that impinge upon learning and exploration. As unique and ever-changing beings, our energies may come together at times in our lives for very specific reasons. We may love one another for a time and then find that our souls' experience must take us down divergent paths.

Although this may cause us sorrow, we must focus on the larger picture. If we devote ourselves to living in our highest purpose we can avail ourselves of the joyful bliss of soulful relationship. This does not imply that this energy will last throughout our lives. There is no contract that ensures two souls will resonate till death do them part.

If change is a constant, then soulful partnership embraces the winds of change. Change creates new opportunities and is an ally of conscious relationship.

JUST PASSING THROUGH

In the mid-nineteenth century an elderly Jewish man living in Boston decided to make a very long and arduous passage to Eastern Europe to pay homage to a great and learned rabbi that he had read about. This man traveled by boat and other means of conveyance for many weeks before finally reaching his destination. After knocking on the rabbi's door, he was greeted by a servant who ushered him up some stairs to the rabbi's room. The rabbi greeted him at the door and welcomed him in. As he looked around the room, he was astonished at the simple and Spartan surroundings. There was but a bed, a chair and a writing desk. He confessed his confusion to the rabbi and asked, "Rabbi, how can it be that such a great and learned man lives in such a manner?" The rabbi reflected briefly and asked his guest, "I see you have but one suitcase, why is that?" He answered, " But rabbi, I'm just passing through." The rabbi responded, "So am I, so am I."

And so are we all. In the illusion of permanence, we fight to keep what is ours. It was never ours. We don't own one another. The more that we open to the impermanence of all things, the more we can permit life to unfold. Soulful relationship can only be born in the loving presence of the moment, without conditions and qualifications. Once we set parameters and permit social restrictions to inhibit our soul's exploration, we close our eyes to the incredible unfolding of life. The joy of the soul is exploration and the more that two people can encourage one another to flower and expand, the more they may resonate in one another's company.

Margaret Mead, the renowned anthropologist, reportedly stated that she had three successful marriages. She said that she was married to three wonderful men; each suited her through different passages of her life. Rather than denigrate her soulful purpose to the societal dictate of anger and hostility around divorce, she maintained her higher being. In such a manner we can see that we may honor our soul's energy. This perspective does not, in fact, encourage easier departure from the commitment of relationship. It simply honors the essence of the relationship rather than the form, and in this manner encourages love energy to come forth and thrive.

COMMITMENT

We ordinarily view commitment as a promise to the outcome. The commitment in marriage is that we will stay married. When we commit to the outcome we tend to dishonor the process. Do we commit to telling the truth, devoting ourselves to intimacy, sharing our visions, increasing our consciousness? If we devoted ourselves to the mastery of the process and toward increasing our authenticity as humans, the integrity of the relationship would most likely produce a more thriving environment.

When we make vows as to the result and ignore the process, we are deluding ourselves. There is no outcome, only the reality of any particular moment. And it is there that our focus must be. For in committing to the process we are ensuring a healthier result.

It has been suggested that the marriage of the future might be with an option to renew every five years or so. Some might protest this, saying that this treats the institution of marriage it in a very flippant manner. Actually, it's quite the opposite. It honors the spirit of marriage.

The concept of a renewable marriage might have a beneficial effect on the relationship. By assuming that the marriage contract protects the relationship, the tendency is to be content sleepwalking through life. "I'm married, I don't need to work at it," becomes the inherent belief. Once again the commitment is to the form rather than the content of the relationship. We're back in that old myth that tells us that all we have to do is be married to be happy, there's no work to be done. But with a shift in how we view commitment, we might very well redirect the energies toward the vitality of the relationship.

If either person could simply decline to renew the contract, without all of the incumbent justifications and blame so inherent in the system of divorce, it might attract our attention to the fundamentals of soulful relationship. Commitment would no longer be lip service, but a highly motivational tool that honored the sanctity of the relationship. If we lived our relationships as though they were renewable, we would be more inclined to stop taking them for granted and honor the profound nature of love. In this manner our relationships might serve as a vessel for our joy and happiness rather than an excuse for our discontent. This is a commitment to sharing our truths and living in our highest purpose.

SOULFUL SEX

There is an inclination to perceive sex as separate from the rest of our lives. There is probably little else that causes as much confusion and ambivalence as sex. Much of our emotional turmoil and dissatisfaction is manifested in our sexual relations. Typically sex is experienced through the limitations of our personality. At times it is guarded and defensive, at other times angry and aggressive. It is often a mechanical release fraught with disappointments consistent with soul-less relationship.

Our anxieties and our dramas are played out sexually. Sex is often a vehicle for the control issues of the relationship. It is a reward for good behavior or an acceptable means of ending an argument.

Although much instruction abounds in regard to improving our sex lives, it is typically devoted to discussion of technique, as though sex were a function of the body alone, separate from the heart and soul.

Sex cannot become soulful without intimacy. They are integrally connected. Each thrives upon all of the tenets of relationship that we have explored. Sex is not meant to be an experience grounded in the result. It often resembles other matters of our lives. Mundane sex tends to be hurried, perfunctory and performance-oriented. It has been relegated to the same process of standardization as the rest of our lives. Our sexual desires typically exceed our sexual satisfaction due to the self-imposed limitations of our sexual encounters.

Soulful sex is as much about being as it is about doing. Lovemaking of this nature glows as much in the aftermath as in the frenzied heat of the orgasmic ride. It permits us to be loved in the splendor of our nakedness, masks no where in sight. Ordinary sex instructs us to keep our eyes closed, as though the act of not seeing somehow enables us to move beyond our inhibitions. With our eyes closed we are separate from our lover, having sex but not partaking in soulful sex. Without complete vulnerability, sex is a physical function, pleasurable yet without the ecstasy of a soulful union.

Soulful sex honors the eyes as the windows of the soul. A lover's eyes penetrating your own, brimming with love and smoldering with lust. The exhilaration of synthesizing intimacy and passion is expressed in your eyes; this is the vessel through which we join. This merging of sexual energy is an *extraordinary* experience.

Soulful sex is deeply spiritual, rooted in the profound sharing of two souls. The path toward soulful sex is to be found through unmasking and vulnerability. It is an exploration of fantasy, desire and love grounded in the absence of judgment or fear. Soulful sex is complete and reckless abandon. There are no expectations and no rules. Two people bathed in the ecstasy of their loving vulnerability, sharing and experimenting with their bodies for the sole purpose of pleasure. Soulful sex is the most extraordinary expression of two souls communicating their love through sexual delight.

With energies harmonized, the means by which two people communicate sexually is an ethereal experience grounded in sexual joy. Surrendering to pleasure, resonating with yourself and your lover, unencumbered by the constraints of fear, guilt and shame dissolve. There is a desire to fill our partner with all of us, the purest expression of unselfishness. Our lover's ecstasy is our own. Our energies are now merged; there is no distinction between their pleasure and ours. We love ourselves for loving another completely. Nothing is held back. This is heaven on earth as we transcend the ordinary and experience the extraordinary.

We feel our energy expanding as we surrender to the bliss of our purpose. Our desires and rhythms fall into an intuitive dance. Separateness dissolves. There is no need to tell your lover what feels good or what you desire; they know at once, as do you. You are each part of the same whole, two souls fully engaged in sexual union. This may well be the peak experience of life.

Soulful lovemaking impacts every nuance of our being. This incredible energy transforms the essence of our relationship. Once having experienced the boundless joy of spiritual sex, our relationship moves into a new realm. The boundaries that melt away during our lovemaking no longer need revisit us. Our relationship now embraces our spiritual energy, free of fear and the illusion of separateness. In this manner, soulful sex is not only a journey of pleasure; it is an exploration into new heights of conscious relationship.

Lovemaking need not be limited to physical sexuality. When soulfully connected, our words can stir our passion in a very powerful way. When we share our most private thoughts and feelings through the expression of language, we are indeed making love. We utilize words to convey the rapture of our hearts, and long after the frenzy of the sexual passion fades, the lovemaking continues through the words passing our lips. Love is shared feeling.

Soulful relationship is a profound feeling of coming home. It's as if we have stepped back into the womb, but with our eyes wide open and our love energy emanating. Loving another soulfully leaves us fuller than we ever imagined. The feeling is one of wonderful peace and contentment, as though there is no safer place in the universe. Yet at the same time it is incredibly exciting. We are completely alive in this state, co-creating new realities every moment. Each instant is a lifetime as we become fully purposeful and attentive. The blending of safety and excitement is unique to the energy of soulful relationship and soulful sex. It is what we all yearn for. It is our destiny. Loving intimacy, soulful sex and extraordinary joy can be ours when we commit to learning, self-mastery and love.

Life is an adventure. Live it without regrets.

THE INVITATION

by Oriah Mountain Dreamer, Indian Elder

It doesn't interest me what you do for a living.
I want to know what you yearn for, and if you dare to
dream of meeting your heart's longing.

It doesn't interest me how old you are.
I want to know if you will risk looking like a fool for love,
for your dreams, for the adventure of being alive.

It doesn't interest me what planets are squaring your moon.
I want to know if you have touched the center of your sorrow,
if you have been opened by life's betrayals or have
become shriveled and closed from fear of further pain.
I want to know if you can sit with pain, mine or your own, without
moving to hide it or fade it or fix it.

I want to know if you can be with joy, mine or your own,
if you can dance with wildness and let ecstasy fill you to the tips
of your fingers and toes without cautioning us to be careful, be
realistic, or to remember the limitations of being human.

It doesn't interest me if the story you're telling me is true.
I want to know if you can disappoint another to be true to yourself, if
you can hear the accusation of betrayal and not betray your own soul.
I want to know if you can see beauty even when it is not pretty every
day, and if you can source your life from God's presence.
I want to know if you can live with failure, yours and mine, and still
stand on the edge of a lake and shout to the silvery moon, "Yes."

It doesn't interest me where you live or how much money you have.
I want to know if you can get up after a night of grief and
despair, weary and bruised to the bone, and do what needs to be
done for the children.

It doesn't interest me who you are or how you came to be here.
I want to know if you will stand in the center of the fire with me
and not shrink back.

It doesn't interest me where or what or with whom you've studied.
I want to know what sustains you from the inside
when all else falls away.
I want to know if you can be alone with yourself, and if you truly
like the company you keep in the empty moments.

NOTES

Introduction
Erich Fromm, *The Art of Loving* (NY: Harper Collins, 1956).
Denise Bretonand and Christopher Largent, *The Paradigm Conspiracy*
(Center City: Hazelden, 1996), pp. 17-19.

Chapter 3
Neale Donald Walsch, *Conversations with God*
(NY: G.P. Putnamís Sons, 1996), p. 123.

Chapter 4
Roger Main, *Jung on Synchronicity and the Paranormal*
(Princeton: Princeton University Press, 1997), p. 93.

Chapter 5
David Deutsch, *The Fabric of Reality* (NY: Penguin Books, 1997),
pp. 262-263.
Albert Einstein, Correspondence Einstein-Michele Beso 1903-1955
(Paris: Hermann, 1972).

Chapter 7
Melba Colgrove, *How to Survive the Loss of a Love* (CA: Prelude Press, 1991).
Gregory Bateson, *Mind and Nature: A Necessary Unity* (NY: E.P. Dutton, 1979), p. 17.
Genevieve Rodis-Lewis, "Limitations of the Mechanical
Model in the Cartesian Conception of the Organism" In Hooker,
Michael, ed. *Descartes* (Baltimore: Johns Hopkins University Press, 1978).
Margaret Wheatley and Myron Kellner-Rogers, *A Simpler Way* (San Francisco:
Berrett-Koehler Pub, 1996), p. 49.
Richard Barrett, *A Guide to Liberating your Soul* (Alexandria, VA: Fulfilling
Books, 1995), pp. 36-38.
Nick Herbert, *Elemental Mind* (NY: Penguin Books, 1994), pp. 10-11.
David Bohm, *Thought as a System* (London: Rutledge, 1994), p. 97.
R.W. Clark, *Einstein the Life and Times* (NY: World Publishing Co., 1971), p. 159.
Fritjof Capra, *The Turning Point* (NY: Simon & Schuster, 1982), p. 83.
(Regards reference to Einstein debate and John Bell).

Chapter 8
Peter Senge, *The Fifth Discipline* (NY: Currency & Doubleday, 1990), Ch. 9,11

INDEX